Chocolate

[chaw-kuh-lit, chawk-lit, chok-] *(pl -s), noun*

....

100 essential recipes

Chocolate

[chaw-kuh-lit, chawk-lit, chok-] *(pl -s), noun*

100 essential recipes

spruce

An Hachette UK Company
www.hachette.co.uk

First published in Great Britain in 2013 by Spruce
A division of Octopus Publishing Group Ltd
Endeavour House, 189 Shaftesbury Avenue, London, WC2H 8JY
www.octopusbooks.co.uk
www.octopusbooksusa.com

Distributed in the US by Hachette Book Group USA
237 Park Avenue, New York NY 10017 USA

Distributed in Canada by Canadian Manda Group
165 Dufferin Street, Toronto, Ontario, Canada M6K 3H6

ISBN 978 1 84601 422 2

Printed and bound in China

10 9 8 7 6 5 4 3 2 1

CONSULTANT PUBLISHER Sarah Ford
COPY EDITOR Alison Copland / Nicole Foster
DESIGN Eoghan O'Brien & Clare Barber
ILLUSTRATOR Abigail Read
PRODUCTION Sarah Kramer

CONTENTS

INTRODUCTION

Who doesn't like chocolate? It is one of our favorite foods, whether it is baked in a rich pudding, swirled into a cool dessert, or eaten in its purest form. We are becoming increasingly fussy about the quality of chocolate and are ever more willing to experiment with the way we cook it. Much of the success in chocolate cookery results from a knowledge of its unique qualities when melted or shaped, particularly for decorative cakes and desserts.

ABOUT CHOCOLATE

Chocolate comes from the cocoa tree, which grows in humid, tropical regions around the Equator. The large cocoa beans are harvested and left to ferment before being dried and shipped abroad. Fermenting is an important part of the production process because this is when the flavor develops, and cocoa beans that are fully fermented produce the best-quality chocolate. After roasting, the

beans undergo various treatments to produce cocoa solids, which are the basic ingredient of all chocolate products, and it is the production process that determines the quality of the chocolate. When you buy dark or milk chocolate, remember that the higher the proportion of cocoa solids, the purer the chocolate will be.

TYPES OF CHOCOLATE

There is an increasingly extensive range of chocolate available for both cooking and eating. The darkest chocolate contains 80% or more cocoa solids and has an intensely chocolaty (though not necessarily bitter) flavor because of its lower sugar content. Perfect for those who prefer a less sweet, richer flavor, it is also the best for use in savory chocolate recipes. Slightly sweeter is dark chocolate that contains 60–70% cocoa solids. This has a dense chocolaty flavor and is a good "all-rounder," ideal for recipes in this book that are made with dark chocolate. It melts well to a smooth, glossy texture

and retains its full flavor. Less expensive brands of dark chocolate contain 30–40% cocoa solids. These are acceptable in family puddings and cakes, but you might like to splash out on the purer chocolate for special occasions.

Milk chocolate is considerably sweeter than dark chocolate and has added milk, sugar, and flavorings, such as vanilla. It contains 20–30% cocoa solids. Again, use the percentage of cocoa solids as a guide when you are buying.

White chocolate contains no solids. Instead, it is made with cocoa butter (the edible fat that is extracted from the beans during processing), milk, sugar, and flavoring.

Unsweetened cocoa, a by-product of the processing method, has a strong, bitter flavor. Good for intensifying the flavor of chocolate, it should always be cooked and needs additional sweetening.

Never use chocolate-flavored cake covering, which is usually sold alongside baking products in supermarkets. It is an imitation chocolate-flavored bar of sugar, vegetable oils, and flavorings.

MELTING CHOCOLATE
ON THE STOVETOP

Break the chocolate into pieces and put them in a heatproof bowl. Rest the bowl over a pan of very gently simmering water, making sure that the base of the bowl does not come into contact with the water. Once the chocolate starts to melt, turn off the heat and leave it until it is completely melted, stirring once or twice until no lumps remain. It is crucial that no water gets into the bowl while the chocolate is melting—steam from the pan, for example—because this will make the melted chocolate solidify. When you are pouring the melted chocolate onto paper for making chocolate decorations, wipe the base of the bowl with a cloth as soon as you take it from the heat, so that no condensed steam drips into the chocolate.

IN THE MICROWAVE

Use a microwave-proof bowl and melt the chocolate on medium power in 1-minute spurts, checking frequently.

IN THE OVEN

Put the chocolate in a small ovenproof bowl or dish and leave the bowl in a low oven, 225°F, checking frequently. Alternatively, put it in an oven that has been switched off after being used for baking.

WITH OTHER INGREDIENTS

Butter, cream, milk, alcohol, or water can be melted with chocolate (see individual recipes). Because of the high fat or sugar content of butter and alcohol, note that the melting time will be reduced.

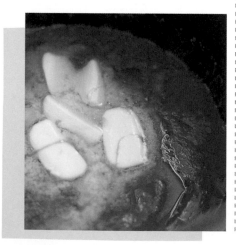

TEMPERING CHOCOLATE

The technique of heating and cooling chocolate before use is known as tempering. It is not essential for any of the recipes in this book, and certainly not necessary when you are adding chocolate to cakes and bakes. It does, however, give a glossy finish and better texture to chocolate that is used for molded shapesor for decorations and confectionery. It also prolongs the keeping quality of chocolate candies and reduces the risk of discoloration or "bloom" dulling the surface. Chocolatiers temper chocolate to precise temperatures using a thermometer and working on a marble slab with a scraper. Here is an easier, quicker way to temper chocolate. Break the chocolate into pieces and melt over a pan of simmering water (see page 7). Remove the bowl from the heat and leave to cool. This will take at least 30 minutes. Stir the melted chocolate gently and frequently as it cools, until it starts to thicken. Return the bowl to the heat and reheat the chocolate very gently so that it thins down but does not completely melt. You can use the tempered chocolate now or leave it over the heat until you are ready.

USING CHOCOLATE AS DECORATIONS

Chocolate can be grated, curled, scribbled, or melted, and modeled into almost any shape. Some techniques take a matter of minutes, while other more imaginative, sculptural forms—the chocolate cases on page 112, for example —require a little more patience and planning. Once made, chocolate decorations keep well in a cool place for up to a week. For special cakes and desserts, you might prefer to temper the chocolate first (see above).

CHOCOLATE CARAQUE

These professional-looking curls take a little effort but are well worth making for a special cake or dessert. They will keep well in the refrigerator for several weeks, or in the freezer for longer. Spread melted chocolate in a thin layer on a marble slab or a clean, smooth surface, such as a new, plastic cutting board or sturdy baking sheet. Allow to set. Holding a knife at an angle, draw it across the chocolate so that you scrape off curls. If the chocolate is too soft and does not curl, pop it in the refrigerator for a few minutes. If it is brittle and breaks off in thin shards, leave it at room temperature for a while before trying again.

CHOCOLATE SHAVINGS

To make more elaborate curls for special cakes and desserts, melt 10 oz dark or white chocolate with 2 tablespoons (¼ stick) unsalted butter. Turn the mixture into a clean butter or margarine tub, and leave until set but not brittle. Remove from the tub and pare off shavings. Protect the end of the slab with foil to prevent the heat of your hand melting the chocolate.

CHOCOLATE SCRIBBLES

Line a tray with nonstick parchment paper. Fill a paper pastry bag with a little melted chocolate and snip off the merest tip. "Draw" shapes on the paper— scribbled lines, curvy swirls, or filigree patterns—and let set. Peel the paper away from the scribbles and use them to decorate chilled desserts. Don't make the patterns too delicate or they will break.

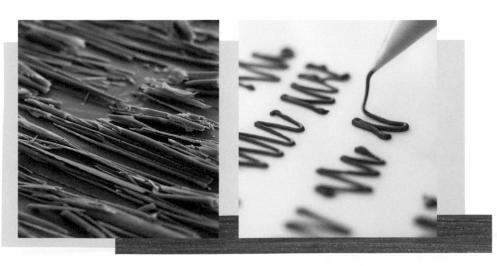

CUT-OUTS

Use small cookie or cake cutters (available from specialist shops) to make shapes for decorating cakes and desserts. Spread melted chocolate on a tray lined with nonstick parchment paper. Allow it to set, then press out the shapes with the cutters. These are good decorations for younger children to experiment with.

EQUIPMENT
FROSTING SPATULAS

These are essential tools for achieving a smooth, even coverage of frosting or ganache. You will need both large and small spatulas, depending on the size of the cake. They are also useful for spreading melted chocolate thinly on paper to make decorations.

COOL SURFACE

A marble slab is the best surface for setting chocolate caraque and other chocolate decorations. A small one that is not too heavy is ideal, because you can put it in the refrigerator to speed up setting. If you haven't got a marble slab but need another firm surface that you can put in the refrigerator so that decorations can firm up, use a thoroughly clean wooden chopping board (preferably one kept for fruit and sweet dishes) or a thick plate or glass board or tray.

DIPPING FORK

Use a long, thin-pronged fork for dipping fruits and sweets into chocolate so that the chocolate does not clog up the tines but drips back into the bowl.

CHOCOLATE RIBBONS

Cut out several 6- × 1¼-inch strips of nonstick parchment paper. Spread melted chocolate over the strips, taking it almost to the edges. Arrange about six small wooden spoons, pens, or chunky pencils in a row and spaced slightly apart on a small tray. Lift the chocolate strips over them so that they set in ribbony waves. Allow to set, then carefully peel away the paper.

JAGGED CHOCOLATE BRITTLE

Spread melted chocolate on a tray or baking sheet lined with nonstick parchment paper. If you like, scatter some finely chopped toasted nuts over the chocolate, chill until really brittle, then peel away the paper and snap the chocolate into jagged shards. Spear into chocolate desserts and special-occasion cakes.

METAL MOLDS

Small metal molds are perfect for individual portions of puddings and desserts and are used in several recipes in this book. Traditional "pudding-shaped" molds have a capacity of about ¾ cup, and the slightly smaller, straight-sided dariole molds have a capacity of about ½ cup. The two are interchangeable in recipes, but bear in mind that rich chocolate desserts are often better in smaller molds.

PAPER PASTRY BAGS

Paper bags are perfect for piping scribbled chocolate decorations directly onto cakes and desserts, or onto paper for setting. To make a paper pastry bag, cut out a 10-inch square of wax paper or nonstick parchment paper and fold it diagonally in half to make a triangle. Cut along the folded line. Holding the center of the long edge toward you, curl the right-hand point of the triangle over to meet the center point, forming a cone. Bring the left-hand point over the cone so that the three points meet. Fold the paper over several times at the points to stop the paper unraveling. Half-fill the bag with melted chocolate and fold down the open end to secure the bag before snipping off the tip. Test the flow and snip off a little more for a thicker flow. If the chocolate sets in the bag before you have had a chance to use it, pop it briefly into the microwave until softened.

ROCKY ROAD TART P44

HOT & COLD DESSERTS

HOT CHOCOLATE & KAHLUA RISOTTO

Chocolate risottos are smooth, creamy, and comforting but chic enough for a casual dinner party if served in small cappuccino cups.

SERVES 4
- 1¾ cups milk
- 1 tablespoon superfine sugar
- ⅔ cup risotto rice
- 4 tablespoons Kahlua or other coffee liqueur
- 5 oz dark chocolate, roughly chopped
- 1 tablespoon chocolate coffee beans, crushed
- Crème fraîche, or sour cream and whipping cream, to serve

1. Put the milk in a large heavy-bottom saucepan with the sugar and heat until it is almost beginning to boil. Sprinkle in the rice, stirring, then reduce the heat to a very gentle simmer.

2. Cook the risotto gently for about 15 minutes, stirring frequently, until it is creamy and the rice has softened but still retains a nutty texture. (If the risotto becomes dry before the rice is cooked, add a splash more milk.)

3. Stir in the liqueur and half the chocolate and stir until the chocolate has melted. Quickly stir in the remaining chocolate and ladle into small, warmed bowls or coffee cups. Scatter with the coffee beans and serve with crème fraîche for swirling into the risotto.

CHOCOLATE PUDDLE PUDDING

- -

This delicious oven-baked pudding separates while baking to produce a gooey chocolate sauce under a light, spongy crust. Serve it hot, well dusted with unsweetened cocoa and with plenty of whipped cream.

SERVES 5-6
- 8 oz dark chocolate, broken into pieces
- 1¼ cups milk
- 2 tablespoons brandy (optional)
- 4 tablespoons (½ stick) unsalted butter, softened
- ½ cup plus 2 tablespoons superfine sugar
- 2 eggs, separated
- ¼ cup self-rising flour
- ¼ cup unsweetened cocoa, plus extra for dusting

1. Preheat the oven to 350°F.

2. Put the chocolate in a small saucepan with the milk and heat gently until the chocolate has melted. Stir in the brandy, if using.

3. Beat together the butter and sugar until pale and creamy. Gradually beat in the egg yolks, flour, cocoa, and melted chocolate mixture.

4. Whisk the egg whites in a separate bowl until they hold their shape.

5. Using a large metal spoon, fold a quarter of the egg whites into the chocolate mixture, then fold in the rest of the egg whites.

6. Turn into a 7½-cup pie dish and place the dish in a roasting pan. Pour a 1-inch depth of boiling water into the pan. Bake in the oven for about 35 minutes until a crust has formed.

7. Dust generously with unsweetened cocoa and serve hot with whipped cream.

WICKED CHOCOLATE PUDDING

This is an indulgent steamed pudding for cold winter days. It is rich and chocolaty, and topped with a buttery date and orange sauce.

SERVES 6

- 6 tablespoons (¾ stick) unsalted butter or margarine, softened, plus extra for greasing
- ¾ cup light brown sugar
- Finely grated zest of 1 orange
- 2 eggs
- 1¼ cups self-rising flour
- ¼ cup unsweetened cocoa
- ½ teaspoon baking soda
- 3½ oz milk chocolate, chopped
- Light cream or custard, to serve

Sauce
- ½ cup light brown sugar
- 6 tablespoons (¾ stick) unsalted butter
- 4 tablespoons orange juice
- 6 tablespoons pitted dried dates, chopped

1. Lightly butter the inside of a 6¼ cup pudding mold and line the bottom with a circle of wax paper. Put the butter or margarine, sugar, orange zest, and eggs in a large bowl. Sift the flour, cocoa, and baking soda into the bowl and beat well until creamy.

2. Stir in the chocolate. Turn the mixture into the prepared mold and level the surface. Cover with a double thickness of wax paper and a sheet of foil, securing them under the rim of the basin with string.

3. Bring a 2-inch depth of water to a boil in a large saucepan. Lower in the pudding and cover with a lid. Steam for 1¾ hours, topping up the water occasionally, if necessary.

4. Meanwhile, make the sauce. Put the sugar, butter, and orange juice in a small saucepan and heat gently until the sugar dissolves. Bring to a boil and boil for 1 minute. Stir in the chopped dates and cook for 1 minute. To serve, invert the pudding onto a serving plate and pour the sauce over the top. Serve with light cream or custard.

CHOCO BREAD &
BUTTER PUDDING

SERVES 4

- 4 chocolate croissants
- 4 tablespoons (½ stick) unsalted butter, plus extra for greasing
- ¼ cup superfine sugar
- ¼ teaspoon apple pie spice
- 1¼ cups milk
- 4 eggs
- 1 teaspoon vanilla extract
- Confectioners' sugar, to decorate

1. Preheat the oven to 350°F. Grease a 6¼-cup shallow, round, ovenproof pie dish.

2. Slice the croissants thickly and spread the butter over one side of each cut face of croissant. Stand the croissant slices upright and close together in the dish to completely fill it.

3. Mix the sugar and spice together, then spoon over the croissants and between the gaps. Stand the dish in a large roasting pan.

4. Beat the milk, eggs, and vanilla extract together, then strain into the dish. Let stand for 15 minutes.

5. Pour hot water from the tap into the roasting pan to come halfway up the sides of the pie dish. Bake in the oven for about 25 minutes until the pudding is golden and the custard just set.

6. Lift the dish out of the roasting pan, dust with sifted confectioners' sugar, and serve the pudding warm with a little light cream.

WHITE CHOCOLATE BRIOCHE PUDDING

Once you have tasted this fabulous pudding, you won't want to go back to its culinary roots—a traditional bread and butter pudding.

SERVES 6

- 8 oz white chocolate, broken into pieces
- 2 tablespoons (¼ stick) unsalted butter, plus extra for greasing
- 8 oz brioche, sliced
- 2 cups fresh or frozen raspberries
- 4 eggs
- 2½ cups milk
- 2 tablespoons superfine sugar
- Confectioners' sugar, for dusting

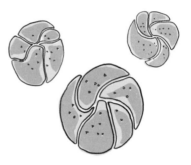

1. Preheat the oven to 375°F. Butter the sides of a shallow 10½-cup ovenproof dish.

2. Melt the chocolate with the butter (see page 7). If the brioche came from a large loaf, cut the slices into smaller triangles or squares. Lay half the bread slices in the dish and spoon over half the chocolate sauce. Scatter with half the raspberries.

3. Lay the rest of the bread over the top and dot with the remaining sauce and raspberries. Beat together the eggs, milk, and sugar and pour the mixture over the pudding. Let soak for 20 minutes.

4. Bake in the oven for about 30 minutes until the surface is turning pale golden and the custard is very lightly set. Let stand for 10 minutes, then serve dusted with confectioners' sugar.

TIP

- For a festive alternative, you can use the same quantity of Italian panettone instead of brioche.

LOW-FAT CHOCOLATE SOUFFLÉS

SERVES 6

- 2 oz dark chocolate, broken into pieces
- 2 tablespoons cornstarch
- 1 tablespoon unsweetened cocoa
- 1 teaspoon instant espresso powder
- 4 tablespoons golden baker's sugar (or superfine)
- ½ cup plus 2 tablespoons skim milk
- 2 eggs, separated
- 1 egg white
- Butter, for greasing
- 1 tablespoon unsweetened cocoa, sifted, for dusting

1. Preheat the oven to 375°F.

2. Heat the chocolate, cornstarch, cocoa, and coffee powder with 1 tablespoon of the sugar and the milk in a pan over a low heat until the chocolate has melted. Continue heating, stirring all the time until the chocolate mixture thickens. Remove from the heat and cool slightly, then stir in the egg yolks and cover with a piece of nonstick parchment paper.

3. Whisk all the egg whites in a grease-free bowl until softly peaking. Gradually whisk in the rest of the sugar until the eggs are stiffly peaking. Fold one-third of the egg whites into the chocolate mixture, then fold in the rest of the egg whites.

4. Grease six heatproof cups or ramekins, each about ⅔-cup, and spoon in the chocolate soufflé mixture. Bake in the oven on a hot baking sheet for 12 minutes or until the soufflés are puffed up.

5. Dust with unsweetened cocoa and eat immediately.

SUNKEN TORTE WITH ORANGE LIQUEUR CREAM

This chocolate cake rises during baking only to sink again as it cools. Don't be put off—the moist density of the mixture makes it utterly delicious.

SERVES 8

- 8 oz dark chocolate, broken into pieces
- ½ cup (1 stick) unsalted butter, plus extra for greasing
- 1 teaspoon vanilla extract
- 6 eggs, separated
- ½ cup light brown sugar
- 1 cup whole milk yogurt
- Finely grated zest and juice of ½ orange
- 2 tablespoons orange liqueur
- 2 tablespoons confectioners' sugar
- Chocolate curls, to decorate (see page 9)

1. Preheat the oven to 325°F. Grease and line a 9-inch springform or loose-bottom cake pan with wax paper, then grease the paper.

2. Melt the chocolate with the butter (see page 7) and stir in the vanilla extract.

3. Whisk the egg yolks with 7 tablespoons of the sugar in a large bowl for 3–4 minutes until the mixture leaves a trail when the whisk is lifted from the bowl. Fold in the chocolate mixture.

4. Whisk the egg whites in a clean bowl until peaking. Gradually whisk in the remaining sugar. Fold a quarter of the whisked whites into the chocolate mixture to lighten it, then fold in the remainder.

5. Turn into the pan and bake in the oven for 30 minutes or until well risen and springy.

6. Beat together the yogurt, orange zest and juice, liqueur, and confectioners' sugar until smooth, then chill. Cool the cake in the pan for 10 minutes before serving with the orange cream and chocolate curls.

CHOCOLATE NUT CRUMBLE

A perfect pudding for winter comfort. For total indulgence, serve it topped with melting vanilla ice cream or lashings of chocolate custard.

SERVES 4-5

- 1½ cups all-purpose flour
- ½ cup (1 stick) unsalted butter, diced
- ¾ cup raw sugar
- 1¾ lb tart apples
- 1½ oz fresh ginger
- 5 oz dark chocolate, broken into pieces
- 3 tablespoons hazelnuts, roughly chopped

1. Preheat the oven to 375°F.

2. Put the flour and butter in a food processor and blend until the mixture starts to resemble coarse bread crumbs. Add 7 tablespoons of the sugar and blend until evenly mixed.

3. Peel, core, and slice the apples and scatter them in a shallow 7½-cup ovenproof dish. Sprinkle over the remaining sugar. Finely chop the ginger and toss with the sugared apples. Scatter the chocolate over the mixture and push some pieces down into the fruit.

4. Sprinkle the crumble mixture over the apple mixture and scatter over the hazelnuts. Bake in the oven for about 40 minutes or until turning golden. Let stand for 10 minutes before serving.

CHOCOLATE & SPICED APPLE STRUDEL

- - - - - - - - - - - - - - - - - -

SERVES 8

Filling
- 2 lb tart apples
- 2 tablespoons lemon juice
- 4 tablespoons (½ stick) unsalted butter, plus extra for greasing
- 1 cup bread crumbs
- 1 teaspoon apple pie spice
- ¼ cup raw sugar
- ⅓ cup golden raisins
- ⅓ cup walnut pieces
- 4 oz dark chocolate, chopped

To finish
- 6 sheets phyllo pastry
- 4 tablespoons (½ stick) unsalted butter, melted
- Confectioners' sugar, for dusting
- Clotted or whipped cream, to serve

1. Preheat the oven to 375°F. Lightly grease a large baking sheet with slightly raised sides.

2. Peel, core, and slice the apples and put in a bowl of water with the lemon juice to prevent discoloration.

3. Melt the butter in a skillet and fry the bread crumbs for about 3 minutes until golden. Drain the apples and add to the pan with the remaining filling ingredients.

4. Lay one sheet of phyllo pastry on the work surface and brush with a little of the butter. Cover with another sheet and brush with more butter. Add a third sheet and spoon half the filling down the center of the pastry to within 1 inch of the edges.

5. Fold the two short ends over the filling, then roll up the pastry like a jelly roll, starting from a long side. Transfer to the baking sheet with the join underneath.

6. Use the remaining pastry, filling, and butter to make a second strudel. Bake in the oven for about 30 minutes until golden. Cool slightly, dust with confectioners' sugar, and serve sliced with clotted or whipped cream.

CHOCOLATE PANCAKE STACK WITH RUM BUTTER

There are many simple variations you can try on this quick and easy pudding. White or dark chocolate, grated orange, or walnuts are equally good in the pancakes, while brandy or an orange-flavored liqueur can be used in the butter.

SERVES 4-6

Rum butter
- 6 tablespoons (¾ stick) unsalted butter, softened
- ½ cup confectioners' sugar
- 3 tablespoons rum

Pancakes
- 3¼ cups plus 2 tablespoons self-rising flour
- 2 tablespoons unsweetened cocoa
- ½ teaspoon baking powder
- 2 tablespoons superfine sugar
- 1 egg
- ¾ cup milk
- 4 oz milk chocolate, roughly chopped
- 3 tablespoons golden raisins
- ¼ cup slivered or flaked almonds
- Oil, for pan-frying

1. Make the rum butter. Beat the butter in a bowl until soft. Add the confectioners' sugar and the rum and beat together until pale and creamy. Transfer to a serving dish.

2. Make the pancakes. Sift the flour, cocoa, and baking powder into a bowl. Add the sugar. Make a well in the center, then add the egg and a little of the milk.

3. Whisk the mixture to make a stiff batter, then beat in the remaining milk. Stir in the chocolate, golden raisins, and almonds.

4. Heat a little oil in a large skillet or griddle. Take spoonfuls of the batter, making sure you scoop up some fruit, nuts, and chocolate each time, and spoon into the pan.

5. Fry gently until just firm and browned on the underside. Turn the pancakes and cook for an additional 1 minute. Drain and keep warm while cooking the remainder.

6. Stack the pancakes and top with spoonfuls of the rum butter.

CHOCOLATE MINT WAFFLES

These dark chocolate waffles, topped with whipped cream flavored with green speckles of fresh garden mint and finished with fresh raspberries or tiny summer strawberries, capture the very essence of summer.

SERVES 4

- Generous ¾ cup all-purpose flour
- 3 tablespoons unsweetened cocoa
- 1 teaspoon baking powder
- ¼ teaspoon baking soda
- 2 tablespoons superfine sugar
- 2 tablespoons (¼ stick) butter, melted
- 1 egg
- ⅔ cup milk

To finish
- 1 cup heavy cream
- 3 tablespoons superfine sugar
- 3 tablespoons chopped mint, plus extra to decorate
- Fresh strawberries and raspberries
- Sifted confectioners' sugar, for dusting

1. Preheat the waffle machine. Sift the flour, cocoa, baking powder, and baking soda into a mixing bowl, then add the sugar. Mix the butter, egg, and milk together in a separate bowl, then gradually beat into the dry ingredients until smooth

2. Pour the batter into the waffle machine, close the lid, and cook until browned and well risen.

3. Meanwhile, pour the cream into a separate bowl, add the sugar and mint, and whip until the cream forms soft swirls.

4. Transfer the waffles to serving plates. Top with spoonfuls of the cream and a sprinkling of fruit and tiny mint leaves. Dust lightly with sifted confectioners' sugar and serve immediately.

PROFITEROLES

SERVES 4-6

Choux pastry
- 4 tablespoons (½ stick) butter or margarine
- ½ cup plus 2 tablespoons water
- ⅔ cup all-purpose flour, sifted
- 2 eggs, beaten

Filling
- ¾ cup heavy cream, whipped

Bitter chocolate sauce
- 6 oz dark chocolate, broken into pieces
- ½ cup plus 2 tablespoons water
- 1 teaspoon instant coffee powder
- ¼ cup sugar

1. Preheat the oven to 425°F.

2. Melt the butter or margarine in a large pan, add the water, and bring to a boil. Add the flour all at once and beat thoroughly until the mixture leaves the side of the pan. Cool slightly, then beat in the eggs vigorously, a little at a time. Put the mixture into a pastry bag fitted with a plain ½-inch tip and pipe small mounds on a dampened baking sheet.

3. Bake in the oven for 10 minutes, then lower the heat to 375°F and bake for an additional 20–25 minutes, until golden brown. Make a slit in the side of each profiterole and place on a wire rack to cool.

4. Put the cream in a pastry bag fitted with an ⅛-inch plain tip and pipe a little into each profiterole.

5. To make the bitter chocolate sauce, place all the ingredients in a small pan and heat gently until the sugar has dissolved. Bring to a boil and simmer gently for 10 minutes.

6. Pile the profiteroles into a pyramid on a serving dish and pour over the chocolate sauce just before serving.

HOT CHOCOLATE CUSTARD

SERVES 4
- I tablespoon all-purpose flour
- 2 tablespoons unsweetened cocoa
- I cup superfine sugar
- 2 egg yolks, beaten
- 2 cups milk
- I tablespoon brandy
- I tablespoon chopped walnuts
- I tablespoon (⅛ stick) butter
- Chopped walnuts, to decorate
- Vanilla ice cream, to serve

1. Thoroughly mix the flour, cocoa, and sugar in a bowl. Add the egg yolks and gradually whisk in the milk until smooth.

2. Pour the mixture into a heavy-bottom pan and cook, whisking continuously, until the custard boils. Reduce the heat to low and cook for 4–5 minutes, still whisking continuously.

3. Remove the pan from the heat and beat in the brandy, walnuts, and butter until well mixed. Pour the custard into serving dishes and decorate with chopped walnuts. Serve at once, with scoops of vanilla ice cream.

OH-SO-EASY ALMOND TORTE

SERVES 16
- 7 oz dark chocolate
- 5 large eggs
- ½ cup golden baker's sugar (or superfine)
- 1 cup ground almonds
- 1 tablespoon coffee liqueur
- Unsweetened cocoa, for dusting
- 1¾ cups fresh raspberries

1. Preheat the oven to 325°F.

2. Melt the chocolate (see page 7).

3. Separate all but one of the eggs, reserving the whites. Whisk the remaining whole egg, egg yolks, and sugar in a bowl until the mixture is pale and creamy and leaves a trail when the beaters are lifted.

4. Whisk in the melted chocolate slowly and then add the almonds. Clean the beaters and whisk the egg whites until softly peaking. Whisk a quarter of the egg whites into the mix to loosen it, then fold in the rest.

5. Grease and line a round cake pan, 5 inches in diameter and 3½ inches deep, ensuring the nonstick parchment paper comes about 3 inches above the pan. Pour the mixture into the pan and bake in the oven for 1–1¼ hours or until a toothpick inserted into the center of the cake comes out clean.

6. Make several holes in the cake while still hot and drizzle over the coffee liqueur. Cool in the pan for 30 minutes. To serve, place the cake on a stand, dust with unsweetened cocoa, top with a pile of raspberries, and wrap a wide ribbon around it.

CHOCOLATE CRÈME BRÛLÉE

SERVES 6

- 2¼ cups heavy cream
- 1 vanilla bean, split in half lengthwise
- 5 oz dark chocolate, broken into pieces
- 6 egg yolks
- 2 tablespoon golden baker's sugar (or superfine)
- 1 tablespoon vanilla sugar
- 4 tablespoons brandy
- 6 tablespoons clotted or whipped cream
- ¼ cup dark brown sugar

1. Heat the heavy cream gently with the vanilla bean until boiling. Remove from the heat, remove the vanilla bean, and add the chocolate. Stir until melted.

2. Whisk together the egg yolks and both types of sugar with the brandy, until the mixture becomes thick, foamy, and pale. Gradually pour on the chocolate cream and whisk in, then strain back into the cleaned pan. Gently heat the mixture, stirring continuously until it has become thick and smooth.

3. Fill six heatproof glass espresso cups with the chocolate custard, then chill for at least 2 hours. Spoon a dollop of clotted cream onto each cup. Sprinkle the top of each cup with dark brown sugar, then use a chef's blowtorch or hot broiler to caramelize the sugar.

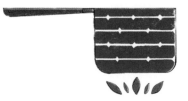

TRIPLE CHOCOLATE BRÛLÉE

SERVES 6

- 8 egg yolks
- ½ cup plus 2 tablespoons golden baker's sugar (or superfine)
- 2½ cups heavy cream
- 4 oz dark chocolate, finely chopped
- 4 oz white chocolate, finely chopped
- 4 oz milk chocolate, finely chopped
- 3 tablespoons Amaretto di Saronno or brandy (optional)
- Dark, milk, and white chocolate curls (see page 9), to decorate (optional)

1. Mix the egg yolks and half the sugar in a bowl, using a fork. Pour the cream into a pan and bring almost to a boil. Gradually beat the cream into the yolk mixture to make a custard.

2. Strain the custard into a pitcher, then divide equally among three bowls. Stir a different chocolate into each bowl, adding 1 tablespoon liqueur, if using. Stir until melted.

3. Divide the dark chocolate custard between six ramekins. When cool, transfer the dishes to the freezer for 10 minutes to set.

4. Remove the dishes from the freezer. Stir the white chocolate custard and spoon it over the dark layer in the dishes. Return to the freezer for 10 minutes.

5. Remove the dishes from the freezer. Stir the milk chocolate custard and spoon into the dishes. Chill in the refrigerator for 3–4 hours until set. About 25 minutes before serving, sprinkle with the remaining sugar and caramelize with a blowtorch or under a hot broiler. Leave at room temperature until ready to eat, then decorate with chocolate curls, if desired.

CHOCOLATE FIG TATIN

Take a short cut to a delicious tarte tatin by using bought puff pastry, sandwiched with chocolaty layers. Serve warm topped with melting ice cream or crème fraîche.

SERVES 6

- ½ cup grated dark chocolate
- 1 teaspoon apple pie spice
- ½ cup superfine sugar
- 1 lb puff pastry, thawed if frozen
- 6 tablespoons (¾ stick) unsalted butter, plus extra for greasing
- 10 fresh figs, quartered
- 1 tablespoon lemon juice
- Vanilla ice cream or crème fraîche, to serve

1. Preheat the oven to 400°F.

2. Mix together the grated chocolate, spice, and 2 tablespoons of the sugar. Cut the pastry into three evenly sized pieces and roll out each to a circle 10 inches across, using a plate or inverted bowl as a guide.

3. Scatter two rounds to within ¾ inch of the edges with the grated chocolate mixture. Stack the pastry layers so that the chocolate is sandwiched in two layers. Press the pastry down firmly around the edges.

4. Lightly butter the sides of a shallow 9-inch round baking pan, 1½ inches deep. (Don't use a loose-bottom pan.) Melt the butter in a skillet. Add the remainder of the sugar and heat gently until dissolved. Add the figs and cook for 3 minutes or until lightly colored and the syrup begins to turn golden. Add the lemon juice.

5. Tip the figs into the baking pan, spreading them in an even layer. Lay the pastry over the figs, tucking the dough down inside the edges of the pan. Bake in the oven for 30 minutes until well risen and golden. Leave for 5 minutes, then loosen the edges and invert onto a serving plate.

CHOCOLATE & PASSION FRUIT ROULADE

- -

Chocolate roulades have a soft, squidgy texture and a sugary crust, which cracks when it is rolled up so it looks craggy, moist, and appealing.

SERVES 8

- 6 oz dark chocolate, broken into pieces
- 5 eggs, separated
- ½ cup superfine sugar, plus extra to sprinkle
- 4 passion fruit, halved and scooped out
- 4 tablespoons orange curd
- 1 cup heavy cream
- Butter, for greasing
- Chocolate curls, to decorate (see page 9)

1. Preheat the oven to 350°F. Grease and line a 13- x 9-inch jelly roll pan with wax paper, then grease the paper.

2. Melt the chocolate (see page 7).

3. Using an electric whisk, beat together the yolks and sugar for about 3–4 minutes until pale and creamy. Using a metal spoon, fold in the melted chocolate.

4. Whisk the egg whites in a clean bowl until peaking but not stiff. Fold about a quarter of the whisked whites into the chocolate mixture to lighten it, then fold in the remainder. Spread the mixture gently into the corners of the pan.

5. Bake in the oven for about 20 minutes until risen and just firm. Invert the roulade onto a sheet of wax paper sprinkled with superfine sugar and peel away the lining paper. Cover and let cool.

6. Add the passion fruit pulp to the orange curd and mix. Lightly whip the cream.

7. Spread the cream just to the edges of the roulade. Spoon the passion fruit mixture over the top, then roll up the roulade, using the paper. Turn onto a plate, join underneath, and scatter the curls over it.

CHOCOLATE PEAR SLICE

This quick and easy dessert is smart enough to serve for a special occasion, and not too heavy if rich courses have preceded it. It can be prepared in advance and cooked just before serving.

SERVES 6

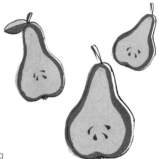

- 5 oz dark chocolate, broken into pieces
- 2 large ripe pears
- 2 tablespoons lemon juice
- 12 oz puff pastry, thawed if frozen
- Beaten egg, to glaze
- Confectioners' sugar, for dusting
- Light cream, to serve

1. Preheat the oven to 400°F. Grease a baking sheet and sprinkle with water.

2. Melt the chocolate (see page 7).

3. Peel, quarter, core, and thinly slice the pears. Put the pear slices in a bowl of water along with the lemon juice. Roll out the pastry on a lightly floured surface to a 12- x 7-inch rectangle, trimming the edges neatly. Using the tip of a sharp knife, make a shallow cut along each side, ½ inch from the pastry edges.

4. Spread the melted chocolate to within ½ inch of the cut line. Thoroughly drain the pears and arrange the slices in overlapping lines over the chocolate, keeping them just inside the cut line. Mark small indentations on the edges of the pastry with the back edge of the knife. Brush the pastry edges with beaten egg, then bake in the oven for about 25 minutes until the pastry is risen and golden. Remove from the oven.

5. Raise the oven temperature to 450°F. Generously dust the pastry and pears with confectioners' sugar and return to the oven for about 5 minutes until deep golden, watching closely. Let cool slightly, then serve warm with light cream.

BLACK FOREST BITES

SERVES 16

- 4 tablespoons (½ stick) lightly salted butter, softened
- ¼ cup light brown sugar
- 1 egg
- ½ cup self-rising flour
- 2 tablespoons unsweetened cocoa
- 3 tablespoons dried sour cherries, chopped

Topping
- 4 oz dark chocolate, chopped
- 2 teaspoons corn syrup
- ⅔ cup heavy or whipping cream
- 2 tablespoons kirsch
- 16 pitted canned black cherries
- 2 tablespoons cherry or red fruit preserves

1. Preheat the oven to 350°F. Place 16 mini silicone cupcake molds on a baking sheet.

2. Put the butter, sugar, and egg in a bowl, sift in the flour and unsweetened cocoa, and beat with an electric hand mixer until pale and creamy. Stir in the sour cherries and divide between the molds.

3. Bake in the oven for 10–12 minutes until risen and just firm. Let cool in the molds for 2 minutes before transferring to a wire rack to cool completely.

4. Make the topping by melting the chocolate (see page 7) and stirring in the syrup. Spoon over the chocolate cakes so the frosting trickles down the sides. Whip the cream with the kirsch and spoon or pipe onto the cakes. Pat the cherries dry on paper towels and place on top of the cakes. If the preserves have a thick consistency, heat in a small saucepan with 2 teaspoons water to soften, then cool slightly before drizzling over the cakes.

5. For glossy chocolate sauce, put ½ cup light brown sugar in a small saucepan with ½ cup water. Heat gently, stirring until the sugar has dissolved, then bring to a boil and boil for 1 minute. Remove from the heat and stir in 1 cup chopped dark chocolate and 2 tablespoons (¼ stick) lightly salted butter. Allow the chocolate to melt, stirring occasionally and returning the pan to the heat if small pieces of chocolate remain. Serve as a warm sauce with the cakes.

WHITE CHOCOLATE & BLUEBERRY TRIFLE

Trifle has a way of reinventing itself, and this version is one of the best. Gin goes perfectly with the fruit and the lemony cream.

SERVES 6-8

- 2½ cups milk
- 4 egg yolks
- 3 tablespoons cornstarch
- 10 oz white chocolate, chopped
- 2½ cups blueberries
- 4 tablespoons gin or vodka
- 4 tablespoons confectioners' sugar, plus extra for dusting
- 10 oz bought or homemade Madeira cake
- 1¼ cups heavy cream
- 2 tablespoons lemon juice
- Dark or white chocolate shavings, to decorate (see page 9)

1. Bring the milk almost to a boil in a medium-sized heavy-bottom saucepan. Beat together the egg yolks and cornstarch in a bowl. Pour the milk over the yolks, stirring, then return the mixture to the saucepan. Cook briefly until the mixture is thickened and bubbling. Stir in the chocolate until melted, and let cool.

2. Reserve ½ cup of the blueberries. Pierce the remainder with a fork and add the liqueur and 2 tablespoons of the confectioners' sugar. Stir, then leave for 5 minutes.

3. Cut the cake into chunks and scatter them in a large glass dish or individual dishes. Sprinkle with the soaked berries, then pile the cooled custard on top.

4. Whip the cream with the remaining confectioners' sugar and the lemon juice until softly peaking. Spoon over the custard. Scatter with the reserved blueberries and chocolate shavings. Serve dusted with confectioners' sugar.

CHOCOLATE AMARETTO DESSERTS

Try these delicious 'grown-up' desserts, laced with almond liqueur. They are set in little jello molds, but you could use small metal dariole molds instead.

SERVES 8

- 1 tablespoon powdered gelatin
- 10 oz dark chocolate, broken into pieces
- ½ cup plus 2 tablespoons Amaretto liqueur
- 1¾ cups milk
- ½ cup heavy cream
- ⅓ cup chocolate syrup

1. Sprinkle the gelatin over 3 tablespoons water in a small bowl and let soak for 5 minutes. Melt the chocolate in a large bowl with the liqueur (see page 7), stirring frequently until smooth.

2. Bring the milk just to a boil and remove from the heat. Pour the warm milk over the chocolate, whisking well until completely smooth.

3. Add the soaked gelatin and stir for 1 minute until dissolved. Divide among eight ½-cup individual molds and let cool. Chill for at least 6 hours, preferably overnight, until just firm.

4. To serve, half-fill a small bowl with very hot water and dip a mold up to the rim in the water for 2 seconds. Invert onto a serving plate and, gripping both plate and mold, shake the dessert out on the plate. Lift away the mold and repeat with the other desserts.

5. Pour a little cream around each dessert, then drizzle a tablespoonful of syrup through it. Lightly swirl the syrup into the cream to decorate.

ETON
MESS

Making the meringues yourself gives by far the best results in this fabulous dessert. You can use good-quality bought ones if you prefer, but avoid the cheap, powdery ones.

SERVES 6
- 2 egg whites
- 7 tablespoons superfine sugar
- ¾ cups heavy cream
- 5 oz white chocolate, chopped
- ¾ cup whole milk yogurt
- 3 cups fresh raspberries

1. Preheat the oven to 275°F. Line a large baking sheet with nonstick parchment paper.

2. Whisk the egg whites in a clean bowl until stiff. Gradually whisk in the sugar, a tablespoonful at a time, whisking well after each addition, until the meringue is stiff and glossy. Put spoonfuls on the baking sheet and bake in the oven for about 1 hour until crisp. Transfer to a wire rack to cool.

3 Make the ganache. In a small saucepan, heat the cream until just bubbling around the edge. Remove from the heat and stir in the white chocolate. Turn into a bowl and stir frequently until the chocolate has melted.

4. Cover and chill until the mixture holds its shape. Mix together the ganache and yogurt. Take three-quarters of the meringues (putting the rest in an airtight container to keep) and crumble them into a large bowl. If they are a bit sticky in the center, just pull them apart. Stir in the raspberries.

5. Add the ganache mixture and lightly fold the ingredients together. Spoon into six glasses and chill until ready to serve.

CHOCOLATE MARBLE CHEESECAKE

When baked, the center of this cheesecake should still feel slightly soft in the middle. Avoid overbaking or the texture will be dry.

SERVES 8-10

- 4 oz gingersnap cookies
- 2 tablespoons unsweetened cocoa
- 3 tablespoons (¼ stick plus 1 tablespoon) unsalted butter

Filling
- 1½ cups cream cheese
- ½ cup plus 2 tablespoons superfine sugar
- 3 eggs
- 2 teaspoons vanilla extract
- ½ cup plus 2 tablespoons heavy cream
- 7 oz dark chocolate, broken into pieces
- light cream, to serve

1. Preheat the oven to 325°F.

2. Put the cookies in a plastic bag and crush them with a rolling pin. Mix the crushed cookies with the unsweetened cocoa. Melt the butter in a small saucepan and stir in the cookie mixture until combined. Press the mixture into the bottom of an 8-inch springform cake pan.

3. Beat the cream cheese to soften, then beat in the sugar, eggs, vanilla extract and cream. Melt the chocolate (see page 7). Spoon about one-third of the cream cheese mixture into a separate bowl and beat in the chocolate.

4. Pour the cream cheese mixture into the pan, then place spoonfuls of the cream cheese and chocolate mixture over it. Using a knife, swirl the mixtures together lightly to create a marbled effect.

5. Bake in the oven for 35–40 minutes or until the center of the cheesecake feels only just set. Turn off the oven and leave the cheesecake to cool in it, then transfer to the refrigerator. Serve chilled with light cream.

ROCKY ROAD
TART

If you want to freeze this tart in advance, cover it closely with plastic wrap and foil once the topping has frozen. Put it in the refrigerator for 30 minutes before serving to soften the topping.

SERVES 8

- 10 oz gingersnap cookies or 20 graham crackers
- ½ cup (1 stick) butter, melted
- 2 tablespoons honey

Filling
- 5 oz honey and almond chocolate
- 1 tablespoon (⅛ stick) butter, melted
- 6 tablespoons heavy cream

- 1¾ cups chocolate ice cream
- 1¾ cups strawberry ice cream
- 1¾ cups vanilla ice cream
- 2 cups mini marshmallows
- ½ cup pecan nuts, roughly chopped
- Fresh cherries or strawberries, to decorate (optional)

1. Put the cookies in a plastic bag and tap them with a rolling pin to make crumbs. Mix the butter, honey, and cookie crumbs together in a bowl. Spoon the mixture into a 10-inch tart pan, pressing it down into the bottom and up the sides with the back of a spoon. Chill for 30 minutes.

2. Melt the chocolate with the butter and cream (see page 7). Leave to one side to cool.

3. Scoop the ice creams onto the cookie base, alternating the flavors as you go. Sprinkle the top with the marshmallows and pecan nuts. Drizzle the tart with the chocolate sauce and freeze it for 2 hours. Decorate with fresh fruit before serving, if liked.

WHITE CHOC & RASPBERRY TIRAMISU

SERVES 6

- 3 level teaspoons instant coffee powder
- 7 tablespoons confectioners' sugar
- 1 cup boiling water
- 12 ladyfingers, about 3½ oz
- 1 cup mascarpone cheese
- ½ cup plus 2 tablespoons heavy cream
- 3 tablespoons kirsch (optional)
- 2 cups fresh raspberries
- 3 oz white chocolate, diced

1. Put the coffee and 4 tablespoons of the confectioners' sugar into a shallow dish, then pour on the boiling water and mix until dissolved. Dip six ladyfingers, one at a time, into the coffee mixture, then crumble into the bases of six glass tumblers.

2. Put the mascarpone into a bowl with the remaining confectioners' sugar, then gradually whisk in the cream until smooth. Stir in the kirsch, if using, then divide half the mixture between the glasses.

3. Crush half the raspberries over the top of the mascarpone in the glasses, then sprinkle with half the chocolate. Dip the remaining ladyfingers in the coffee mix, crumble, and add to the glasses. Then add the rest of the mascarpone and the remaining raspberries, this time left whole, finishing with a sprinkling of the chocolate.

4. Serve immediately or chill until required.

QUICK WHITE CHOCOLATE MOUSSE

SERVES 4
- ½ cup superfine sugar
- ½ cup shelled pistachios
- 7 oz white chocolate, chopped
- 1¼ cups heavy cream

1. Dissolve the sugar with 4 tablespoons water in a small pan over a low heat. Increase the heat and boil until it begins to caramelize. Tip in the pistachios and stir, then pour the mixture onto some wax paper on a baking sheet and let set.

2. Put the chocolate in a heatproof bowl. Heat the cream in a saucepan until it reaches boiling point, then remove from the heat and pour directly over the chocolate, stirring constantly until it has melted. Refrigerate until cold, then beat with an electric hand mixer until thick.

3. Spoon the cold chocolate into serving dishes, decorate with broken shards of the pistachio praline, and serve.

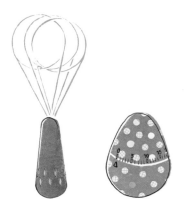

CHOCOLATE & GINGERSNAP MOUSSE

SERVES 4

- I cup dark chocolate, broken into pieces
- 3 tablespoons strong coffee
- 3 eggs, separated
- 10 gingersnap cookies
- 3 tablespoons (¼ stick plus I tablespoon) butter
- 4 tablespoons sour cream
- Sifted instant cocoa

1. Melt the chocolate (see page 7). Stir in the coffee, then gradually mix in the egg yolks one at a time. Let cool slightly.

2. Place the cookies in a plastic bag and crush with a rolling pin to make fine crumbs. Melt the butter in a small saucepan, then stir in the crumbs. Line four ⅔-cup ramekin dishes with plastic wrap so that the wrap overhangs the edges of the dishes. Divide half the crumbs between the bases of the dishes and press flat.

3. Beat the egg whites until soft peaks, then stir a spoonful into the chocolate mixture to loosen it slightly. Fold in the remaining egg whites using a metal spoon. Pour the mousse mixture into the dishes, level the surfaces, then sprinkle with the remaining crumbs.

4. Chill for 4–5 hours or until set.

5. When ready to serve, lift the mousses out of the dishes using the plastic wrap and then peel the plastic wrap away. Top each mousse with a spoonful of sour cream, then decorate with a light dusting of instant cocoa.

RICH MOCHA POTS

This dark, sultry take on chocolate mousse is a sophisticated, grown-up dessert. For best results, use the finest chocolate you can find and chill the mousse well before serving.

SERVES 6-8

- 6 oz dark chocolate, broken into pieces
- 3 tablespoons strong black coffee
- 1 tablespoon (⅛ stick) butter
- 4 eggs, separated
- 2 tablespoons brandy
- 4 tablespoons confectioners' sugar

To decorate
- Whipped cream
- Grated chocolate or curls
  (see page 9)

1. Melt the chocolate (see page 7). Stir in the coffee and butter until smooth.

2. Remove from the heat and whisk in the egg yolks one by one until the mixture is smooth and glossy. Whisk in the brandy, then set aside to cool and thicken slightly while you are whisking the egg whites.

3. Whisk the egg whites in a nonreactive bowl until stiff. Gradually add the sugar and continue whisking until glossy and thick. Fold into the cooled chocolate mixture.

4. Pour into six or eight small teacups or ramekins and chill for 3-4 hours until firm. Top with whipped cream and the grated chocolate or chocolate curls.

TIP

- Recipes using raw eggs should be avoided by infants, the elderly, pregnant women, and anyone with a compromised immune system.

CHOCOLATE AFFOGATO WITH FUDGE SAUCE

Affogato is a wonderful instant dessert—and easy to make to finish any dinner party. Normally a shot of fresh espresso coffee is poured over a scoop or two of vanilla ice cream. Here the addition of a little rich chocolate fudge sauce makes this a real treat.

SERVES 6

- 8 oz dark chocolate (50–70% cocoa solids), broken into pieces
- ⅔ cup light brown sugar
- 1 cup heavy cream
- 2 tablespoons (¼ stick) butter
- 1 tablespoon corn syrup
- 12 scoops good-quality vanilla ice cream
- 6 shots of hot espresso coffee

1. Place the chocolate, sugar, cream, butter, and corn syrup in a saucepan and stir over a gentle heat until the sauce is smooth.

2. Pour the hot chocolate sauce into six sundae glasses or bowls.

3. Place two scoops of vanilla ice cream on top of each and finally pour over the hot coffee. Serve immediately.

TIP

- For a double hit of coffee, substitute the vanilla ice cream with a coffee one. For contrast, add whipped cream on the top. For a different flavor, use maple syrup instead of corn syrup.

CHOCOLATE MAPLE ICE CREAM

- - - - - - - - - - - -

SERVES 4-6

- ¼ cup raisins
- ¼ cup boiling water
- 2 egg yolks
- ¼ cup soft brown sugar
- ⅔ cup dark chocolate, broken into pieces
- 3 tablespoons maple syrup
- 1¼ cups heavy or whipping cream
- Cat's tongue cookies or wafer cookies, for serving (optional)

1. Place the raisins in a bowl and add the boiling water. Soak for 15 minutes, then drain and set aside.

2. In a large bowl, whisk the egg yolks and sugar until pale and creamy. Combine the chocolate and maple syrup in a heatproof bowl and place over a pan of gently simmering water. Stir until the chocolate has melted. Let cool.

3. Place the chocolate and the egg mixture in an ice cream maker, then add the cream. Churn and freeze following the manufacturer's instructions.

4. Once frozen, fold in the raisins. Transfer to a freezer container, cover, and freeze until firm.

5. Transfer the ice cream to the refrigerator 30 minutes before serving to soften slightly. Serve with cat's tongue cookies or wafer cookies, if liked.

DOUBLE CHOCOLATE CHIP ICE CREAM

SERVES 4-6

- 1¼ cups milk
- 6 tablespoons soft dark brown sugar
- 8 oz dark chocolate, broken into pieces
- 2 eggs, beaten
- ½ teaspoon vanilla extract
- 1¼ cups heavy or whipping cream
- ½ cup chocolate chips

1. Put the milk, sugar, and dark chocolate into a saucepan and heat gently until the chocolate has melted and the sugar dissolved. Pour the warm mixture onto the beaten eggs, stirring constantly.

2. Return the mixture to the pan and cook over low heat, stirring constantly, until the custard thickens very slightly. Strain the mixture into a bowl and add the vanilla extract. Let cool.

3. Place the cooled custard in an ice cream maker and add the cream. Churn and freeze following the manufacturer's instructions. Once frozen, stir in the chocolate chips.

4. Serve immediately in individual dishes. Alternatively, transfer the ice cream to a container, cover, and place in the freezer until needed.

TURKISH DELIGHT & CHOCOLATE RIPPLE

Swirling Turkish delight and chocolate sauces into softly set ice cream makes a fabulous concoction for scooping into glasses or ice cream cones.

SERVES 6-8

- 1¼ cups milk
- 4 egg yolks
- 7 tablespoons superfine sugar
- 1 teaspoon cornstarch
- 1¼ cups heavy cream
- 7 oz rose-flavored Turkish delight
- 3½ oz dark chocolate, broken into pieces
- 2 tablespoons (¼ stick) unsalted butter

1. Heat the milk in a medium-sized heavy-bottom saucepan until almost boiling. Beat together the egg yolks, 6 tablespoons of the sugar, and the cornstarch in a bowl. Add the hot milk, stirring. Return the mixture to the pan and cook over a very gentle heat, stirring with a wooden spoon until slightly thickened. Turn the mixture into a bowl, cover with a circle of wax paper, and let cool.

2. Whip the cream until it just holds its shape. Stir it into the cooled custard and turn the mixture into a shallow freezer container. Freeze for 4–6 hours until softly set.

3. Alternatively, if you have an ice cream maker, stir the cream into the custard and churn until softly set. Transfer to a shallow freezer container.

4. Meanwhile, make the sauces. Cut up the Turkish delight with scissors and blend in a food processor with ½ cup cold water. Transfer to a small saucepan and cook gently until smooth and syrupy.

5. Put the chocolate in a small saucepan and add the butter, the remaining sugar, and 2 tablespoons water. Heat gently to make a smooth sauce.

6. When the sauces are cool but still runny, spoon them over the ice cream and fold in until rippled. Re-freeze until firm.

MINT CHOCOLATE CHIP ICE CREAM

SERVES 8
- 2 egg whites
- ⅔ cup superfine sugar
- 13 oz can evaporated milk, chilled
- ½ teaspoon peppermint extract
- 8 oz dark chocolate, finely chopped

1. Lightly whisk the egg whites until they form soft peaks, then gradually whisk in the sugar. Place the evaporated milk in a bowl with the peppermint extract and whisk until thick, then fold into the meringue mixture with the chocolate.

2. Turn into an ice cream maker and churn and freeze following the manufacturer's instructions.

3. Serve immediately in chilled dishes or transfer to a container, cover, and place in the freezer until needed.

CHOCOLATE & MASCARPONE ICE CREAM

SERVES 6

- 1¼ cups superfine sugar
- 1½ cups water
- 3½ cups dark chocolate, finely chopped
- 1 cup chocolate chips
- 1 cup mascarpone cheese
- 2 tablespoons lemon juice
- 1¼ cups whipping cream
- ¼ cup coffee liqueur

1. Put 2 tablespoons of the sugar into a heavy-bottom saucepan with 2/3 cup of the water. Heat gently until the sugar dissolves, then bring to a boil and boil rapidly for 3 minutes. Transfer the syrup to a bowl, stir in the chopped chocolate, and let it melt. (If the syrup cools before the chocolate has melted, heat it briefly in the microwave.)

2. Reserve ⅓ cup of the chocolate chips. Finely chop the remainder. Beat the mascarpone in a bowl until softened. Stir in the lemon juice and the melted chocolate mixture.

3. Place the mascarpone and chocolate mixture in an ice cream maker and then pour in the cream. Churn and freeze following the manufacturer's instructions. Once frozen, fold in the chopped chocolate chips. Transfer the ice cream to a container and place in the freezer while making the coffee syrup.

4. To make the coffee syrup, heat the remaining sugar and the remaining water in a small heavy-bottom saucepan until the sugar dissolves. Bring to a boil and boil for 5 minutes until syrupy. Remove from the heat and stir in the coffee liqueur. Let cool, then chill until ready to serve.

5. Transfer the ice cream to the refrigerator about 30 minutes before serving to soften slightly. Stir the reserved chocolate chips into the syrup. Scoop the ice cream onto serving plates, spoon the coffee syrup over the ice cream, and serve immediately.

CHOCOLATE-SWIRLED RAISIN BREAD P76

CAKES, BAKES, COOKIES & BARS

CHOCOLATE CHERRY CAKE

Sandwiched and topped with white chocolate ganache, this cake makes a lighter alternative to the more familiar dark chocolate and cherry combination.

SERVES 8-10

- 4 eggs
- 7 tablespoons superfine sugar
- 1 teaspoon vanilla extract
- ¾ cup plus 2 tablespoons all-purpose flour
- 6 tablespoons grated white chocolate
- Butter, for greasing

To decorate

- 1½ cups red or black cherries, pitted
- 1¼ cups heavy cream
- 10 oz white chocolate, chopped

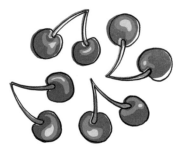

1. Preheat the oven to 350°F. Grease and line the bottoms of two 7-inch round shallow cake pans.

2. Put the eggs, sugar, and vanilla extract in a large heatproof bowl over a pan of hot water and whisk for 6–8 minutes or until the whisk leaves a trail when lifted from the bowl. Remove from the heat and whisk for 2 minutes.

3. Sift the flour into the bowl and sprinkle with the grated chocolate. Fold in gently using a large metal spoon. Divide the batter among the pans and gently level the surface. Bake in the oven for about 25 minutes or until just firm to the touch. Transfer to a wire rack to cool.

4 In a small saucepan, heat the cream until just bubbling around the edge. Remove from the heat and stir in the chocolate. Turn into a bowl and stir frequently until the chocolate has melted.

3. Cover and chill until the mixture holds its shape before spreading. Halve half of the cherries. Spread one cake layer with half the ganache and the cherries on top. Cover with the other cake and spread with the remaining ganache. Scatter with the rest of the cherries and chocolate curls.

ITALIAN UNCOOKED CHOCOLATE CAKE

MAKES 1 X 8-INCH CAKE

- ½ cup plus 2 tablespoons (1¼ sticks) butter, softened, plus extra for greasing
- 1 tablespoon sugar
- 1 tablespoon corn syrup
- 2 tablespoons unsweetened cocoa
- 18 graham crackers, finely crushed
- ¼ cup ground almonds
- 2 teaspoons coffee extract
- 3 oz dark chocolate

1. Grease an 8-inch square cake pan.

2. Cream the butter and sugar in a mixing bowl until pale and creamy. Place the syrup in a saucepan and warm gently over a low heat. Remove from the heat and add the cocoa, crumbs, almonds, and coffee extract. Let cool and stir into the creamed mixture. Press the mixture into the prepared cake pan. Refrigerate for several hours until firm.

3. Melt the chocolate (see page 7). Pour evenly over the cake, tipping the pan to level the topping, then return the cake to the refrigerator until set.

4. Serve in small squares.

COFFEE & CHOCOLATE STREUSEL CAKE

SERVES 16

Topping
- ⅓ cup self-rising flour
- ¼ cup superfine sugar
- 4 tablespoons (½ stick) butter, diced
- ⅓ cup roughly chopped hazelnuts
- ¼ cup slivered almonds
- 3½ oz dark chocolate, cut into chunks
- Sifted confectioners' sugar, to decorate

Cake
- 3 teaspoons instant coffee powder
- 2 teaspoons boiling water
- ¾ cup (1½ sticks) butter, at room temperature
- ¾ cup plus 2 tablespoons superfine sugar
- 3 eggs
- 1⅓ cups self-rising flour
- 1 teaspoon baking powder

1. Preheat the oven to 350°F.

2. Cut a piece of nonstick parchment paper a little larger than a shallow 8-inch square baking pan. Snip diagonally into the corners of the paper, then press the paper into the pan to line the bottom and sides.

3. To make the streusel topping, put the flour, sugar, and butter into a bowl and blend in the butter until it resembles fine crumbs. Stir in the nuts.

4. To make the cake, mix the coffee and boiling water together in a cup until the coffee has dissolved. Cream the butter and sugar together in a large bowl until pale and creamy. In a small bowl, lightly beat the eggs and, in a separate bowl, mix the flour and baking powder together.

5. Gradually beat the eggs and flour alternately into the butter mixture until it has all been added. Continue beating until smooth, then mix in the coffee.

6. Spoon the batter into the lined pan and spread level. Sprinkle with the chocolate and then the streusel mixture. Bake in the oven for 40–45 minutes, until the topping is golden brown and a toothpick inserted into the center of the cake comes out cleanly.

7. Let the cake cool slightly in the pan, then lift out using the lining paper. Peel away the paper, dust with a little sifted confectioners' sugar, and cut into squares. Serve warm or cold.

SACHERTORTE

This famous Austrian cake originates in Vienna, where all the cafés claim to make the best one. Don't be tempted to smooth the top of the finished cake, or it will lose its glossy sheen.

SERVES 8-10

- 6 oz dark chocolate (70% cocoa solids), broken into pieces
- ½ cup (1 stick) butter
- ¾ cup sugar
- 5 eggs, separated
- 1 cup all-purpose flour

Glaze
- 3 tablespoons apricot jelly

Frosting
- ⅔ cup superfine sugar
- 3½ oz dark chocolate (70% cocoa solids), broken into pieces
- 6 tablespoons water

1. Preheat the oven to 325°F. Line an 8-inch cake pan with nonstick parchment paper.

2. Melt the chocolate (see page 7).

3. Beat the butter and sugar together, then beat in the egg yolks. Stir in the melted chocolate.

4. Beat the egg whites to soft-peak stage and carefully fold into the chocolate mixture.

5. Sift the flour over and fold in, trying to keep as much air as possible in the mixture. Spoon into the prepared pan and bake in the oven for 40–45 minutes or until a toothpick inserted into the middle comes out clean. Let cool in the pan, then place on a wire rack.

6. For the glaze, heat the apricot jelly with a tablespoon of water. If lumpy, pass through a strainer. Cool a little, then brush the glaze over the cake.

7. Heat the frosting ingredients in a saucepan until the sugar has dissolved and the chocolate melted. Increase the heat and boil until the mixture reaches 221°F on a candy thermometer. Remove from heat and stir for 1 minute. Pour over the cake and smooth the sides with a spatula.

BAKED CHOCOLATE CHEESECAKE

SERVES 2
- 2 tablespoons (¼ stick) unsalted butter
- 1 cup crushed ratafia cookies
- ⅔ cup cream cheese
- 2 tablespoons superfine sugar
- 3 tablespoons mascarpone cheese
- 2 oz dark chocolate
- 1 egg
- 1 egg yolk

To decorate
- Sour cream
- Chocolate shavings (see page 9)

1. Preheat the oven to 350°F.

2. Melt the butter in a saucepan. Add the crushed cookies and mix well. Divide the mixture among two tart pans, each 4 inches across, and press down to form the cheesecake bases.

3. Place the cream cheese, superfine sugar, mascarpone, and chocolate in a small pan and warm over a gentle heat, stirring until the mixture is melted and blended.

4. Remove from the heat, let cool, then beat in the egg and the yolk.

5. Divide the chocolate mixture among the tart pans, place them on a baking sheet, and bake in the oven for 45 minutes or until set. Remove from the oven and allow the cheesecakes to cool before transferring them to the refrigerator. Chill until required, then decorate with a dollop of sour cream and chocolate shavings.

CHOCOLATE & RASPBERRY ROULADE

- - - - - - - - - - - - - - - - - - -

This is a perfect afternoon tea treat—just sweet and creamy enough to keep you going through the rest of the day.

SERVES 6-8

- 6 oz good-quality dark chocolate, broken into pieces
- ⅓ cup water
- 1 tablespoon instant coffee granules
- 5 eggs, separated
- ⅔ cup superfine sugar
- ¾ cup heavy cream, whipped
- 1¼ cups fresh raspberries
- Confectioners' sugar, for dusting

1. Preheat the oven to 400°F. Line a large 9- x 13-inch jelly roll pan with nonstick parchment paper.

2. Melt the chocolate with the water and coffee (see page 7). Let cool slightly.

3. Combine the egg yolks and superfine sugar and whisk until pale and creamy. Stir in the melted chocolate. Beat the egg whites to soft peaks and carefully fold into the chocolate mixture.

4. Pour into the jelly roll pan and bake in the oven for 10–12 minutes until firm. Turn out onto another piece of parchment paper and cover with a damp dish towel. Let cool.

5. Spread the whipped cream over the sponge, evenly scatter the raspberries on top, and roll up. Dust with confectioners' sugar just before serving.

WHITE CHOCOLATE SUMMER BERRY CAKE

This creamy cake is packed with white chocolate and berries. It can be made a day in advance and assembled a few hours before serving.

SERVES 12

- 5 eggs
- ½ cup plus 2 tablespoons superfine sugar
- 1¼ cups all-purpose flour
- 6 tablespoons grated white chocolate
- 4 tablespoons (½ stick) unsalted butter, melted, plus extra for greasing
- 1½ cups strawberries
- 1½ cups raspberries
- 1¼ cups heavy cream
- 4 tablespoons orange liqueur
- ⅓ cup melted white chocolate

1. Preheat the oven to 350°F. Grease and line the bottoms of two 8-inch round shallow cake pans. Grease the paper.

2. Beat the eggs and sugar in a heatproof bowl over a pan of hot water until the whisk leaves a trail when lifted from the bowl. Remove from the heat and whisk for an additional 2 minutes.

3. Sift the flour over the mixture, sprinkle with the chocolate, and fold in. Drizzle the melted butter over the mixture and fold in. Divide among the pans and bake in the oven for 25–30 minutes or until just firm. Transfer to a wire rack to cool.

4. Reserve a handful of the fruits and lightly mash the remainder. Whip the cream until just peaking. Halve each cake and drizzle with the liqueur. Spread one layer with one-third of the whipped cream and then one-third of the fruits. Repeat the layering, finishing with a cake layer. Spread a little melted chocolate over the cake to seal in any crumbs, then swirl over the remainder. Scatter with the reserved fruits.

WHITE CHOCOLATE & LAVENDER MADEIRA

Light, buttery, and subtly flavored, this is a good teatime cake to make when lavender is coming into bloom.

SERVES 8

- 5 oz white chocolate, broken into pieces
- 8 lavender sprigs
- 2 tablespoons superfine sugar
- ½ cup (1 stick) unsalted butter, softened, plus extra for greasing
- 2 eggs, beaten
- 1 cup self-rising flour
- ¼ cup ground almonds
- Confectioners' sugar, for dusting

1. Preheat the oven to 350°F. Grease and line the bottom and long sides of a 1-lb loaf pan with a strip of wax paper. Grease the paper.

2. Melt the chocolate (see page 7).

3. Pull the lavender flowers from the stalks and beat them in a bowl with the sugar and butter until pale and creamy. (Discard the stalks.) Gradually beat in the eggs, adding a little of the flour to prevent curdling.

4. Stir in the melted chocolate. Sift the remaining flour over the bowl and gently fold in with the ground almonds.

5. Turn the batter into the pan and level the surface. Bake in the oven for 40 minutes until risen and firm to the touch. Transfer to a wire rack to cool and serve generously dusted with confectioners' sugar.

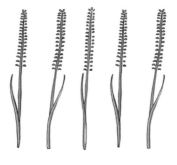

WHITE CHOCOLATE, PEAR & ALMOND CAKE

You could use dried cherries or blueberries instead of the nuts, if you prefer.

SERVES 8-10
- I ripe pear
- ¾ cup plus 2 tablespoons (1¾ sticks) butter, slightly softened, plus extra for greasing
- ¾ cup superfine sugar
- 3 eggs
- 2 teaspoons vanilla extract
- 1½ cups all-purpose flour
- 1 teaspoon baking powder
- 5½ oz white chocolate, finely chopped
- ⅓ cup blanched almonds, roughly chopped
- Confectioners' sugar, for dusting

1. Preheat the oven to 350°F. Grease and line the bottom of an 8-inch cake pan.

2. Peel and core the pear and cut into eighths.

3. Cream the butter and sugar together until pale and creamy. Gradually beat in the eggs and vanilla extract.

4. Fold in the flour and baking powder, and finally the white chocolate and almonds.

5. Spoon the batter into the prepared pan and level the surface. Place the pears in a circle on top, pressing them down into the batter. Bake in the oven for 45–50 minutes or until risen and firm in the center.

6. Let cool in the pan for 10 minutes before removing and cooling on a wire rack. Dust with confectioners' sugar to serve.

WHITE CHOCOLATE CAPPUCCINO CAKE

- -

White chocolate can be a bit sickly but the bitterness of the coffee cuts through the sweetness. This works well sandwiched with slightly sweetened whipping cream, but you could use a frosting of your choice.

SERVES 6-8

- 4½ oz white chocolate, broken into pieces
- 3 tablespoons milk
- ¾ cup (1½ sticks) butter, slightly softened, plus extra for greasing
- ¾ cup light brown sugar
- 3 eggs
- 2 teaspoons instant coffee granules mixed with 2 tablespoons boiling water
- 1½ cups self-rising flour
- ⅔ cup heavy cream
- 1 tablespoon confectioners' sugar, plus extra for dusting

1. Preheat the oven to 350°F. Grease and line the bottoms of two 7-inch round shallow cake pans.

2. Melt the chocolate with the milk (see page 7). Let cool a little, then stir.

3. Cream the butter and sugar together until pale and creamy. Gradually beat in the eggs and then the coffee liquid.

4. Stir in the melted chocolate. Mix well and then finally fold in the flour.

5. Divide the batter among the two pans and bake in the oven for 20–25 minutes until golden and firm to the touch. Turn out onto a wire rack and let cool.

6. When the cake has cooled, whip together the cream and confectioners' sugar until it is holding its shape, and spread over one half of the cake. Top with the remaining half and dust the top liberally with confectioners' sugar.

DRAMBUIE FRUIT CAKE

Adding chocolate to a chunky fruit cake might seem a little overindulgent, but the results are absolutely delicious, particularly if the fruit has been steeped in alcohol before baking.

SERVES 16

- 2 cups golden raisins
- 8 tablespoons Drambuie
- 1 cup (2 sticks) unsalted butter, softened, plus extra for greasing
- 1 cup light brown sugar
- 4 pieces of stem ginger, finely chopped
- 4 eggs
- 1¾ cups all-purpose flour
- ¼ cup unsweetened cocoa
- 1 teaspoon baking powder
- 1 cup unblanched hazelnuts, roughly chopped
- 4 oz dark chocolate, chopped
- 4 oz milk chocolate, chopped

1. Preheat the oven to 300°F.

2. Put the golden raisins and Drambuie in a bowl. Cover and leave for at least 4 hours or overnight. Grease and line the bottom and sides of an 8-inch round cake pan. Grease the paper.

3. Cream together the butter, sugar, and ginger. Gradually beat in the eggs, adding a little of the flour to prevent curdling. Sift the remaining flour into the bowl with the cocoa and baking powder.

4. Reserve 3 tablespoons of the nuts and a quarter of each type of chopped chocolate and stir the remainder into the batter with the raisins and any soaking juices. Stir well until combined. Turn into the pan and level the surface.

5. Scatter with the reserved chocolate and nuts. Bake in the oven for about 1½ hours or until firm and a toothpick inserted into the center comes out clean. Let cool in the pan.

FRUITED CHOCOLATE CAKE

SERVES 12-14

- 1 cup (2 sticks) unsalted butter or margarine, softened, plus extra for greasing
- 1 cup light brown sugar
- 2¼ cups all-purpose flour
- ¼ cup unsweetened cocoa
- 1 teaspoon apple pie spice

- 4 eggs
- 1½ cups roughly chopped mixed nuts, such as Brazil nuts, almonds, and hazelnuts
- 8 oz milk chocolate, chopped
- ½ cup chopped candied ginger
- 1½ cups mixed dried fruit

1. Preheat the oven to 300°F. Grease and line an 8-inch round cake pan.

2. Cream the butter and sugar together in a bowl until softened. Sift the flour, cocoa, and apple pie spice into the bowl. Add the eggs and beat until smooth.

3. Reserve 3 tablespoons of the chopped nuts, a quarter of the chopped chocolate, and half the candied ginger. Add the remainder to the batter with the mixed dried fruit and stir until evenly combined.

4. Turn the batter into the prepared pan and level the surface. Scatter with the reserved nuts, chocolate, and ginger.

5. Bake in the oven for 1¼–1½ hours until a toothpick inserted into the center comes out clean. Let cool in the pan.

RIPPLED CHOCOLATE & BANANA TEABREAD

SERVES 10

- 7 oz dark chocolate, broken into pieces, plus 2 oz, chopped
- ½ teaspoon ground ginger
- ¾ cup plus 2 tablespoons (1¾ sticks) unsalted butter or margarine, softened, plus extra for greasing
- 2 ripe bananas
- ¾ cup superfine sugar
- 3 eggs
- 2 cups self-rising flour
- ½ teaspoon baking powder
- Confectioners' sugar, for dusting (optional)

1. Preheat the oven to 350°F. Lightly grease the bottom and long sides of a 2-lb loaf pan.

2. Melt the 7 oz chocolate with the ginger and 2 tablespoons of the butter or margarine (see page 7).

3. Mash the bananas. Put the remaining butter or margarine in a bowl with the sugar and beat until pale and creamy. Add all the eggs and the banana puree. Sift the flour and baking powder into the bowl. Beat together until smooth.

4. Spread a quarter of the creamed batter into the pan, then spoon over one-third of the chocolate mixture. Spread with another quarter of the batter, then more chocolate. Repeat the layering, finishing with a layer of the batter.

5. Scatter the chopped chocolate down the center of the cake. Bake in the oven for about 1 hour until a toothpick inserted into the center comes out clean. Leave in the pan for 10 minutes before transferring to a wire rack to cool completely. Dust with confectioners' sugar, if liked.

WHITE CHOCOLATE & BANANA LOAF

SERVES 10

- 7½ oz mashed banana (about 2 large bananas)
- ½ cup plus 2 tablespoons warm milk
- 4 tablespoons (½ stick) unsalted butter, softened
- ½ teaspoon salt
- 3½ cups bread flour
- ¼ cup superfine sugar
- 2½ teaspoons instant dried yeast
- 7 oz white chocolate, chopped
- 1 cup pecan nuts, roughly chopped
- Confectioners' sugar, for dusting

1. Lift the bread pan out of your bread-making machine and fit the blade. Put the ingredients, except the chocolate and nuts, in the pan, following the order specified in the manual. Add the mashed banana with the milk.

2. Fit the pan into the machine and close the lid. Set to a 1¼-lb loaf size on the fast/rapid bake program. Add the chocolate and pecans when the machine beeps.

3. At the end of the program, lift the pan out of the machine and shake the bread out onto a wire rack to cool. Serve dusted with confectioners' sugar.

CHOCOLATE-SWIRLED RAISIN BREAD

- -

A deliciously rich and buttery bread to serve for an unhurried weekend breakfast. Make sure the chocolate butter is cool before you spread it over the dough.

SERVES 10

- ½ cup (1 stick) lightly salted butter, plus extra for greasing
- 1 egg
- ½ cup plus 2 tablespoons milk
- 2 teaspoons instant dried yeast
- 3½ cups bread flour
- 1½ teaspoons apple pie spice
- 6 tablespoons golden baker's sugar (or superfine)
- 5 oz dark or milk chocolate, broken into pieces
- ½ cup raisins
- ⅓ cup unblanched hazelnuts, chopped
- Confectioners' sugar, for dusting

1. Preheat the oven to 400°F.

2. Melt 7 tablespoons of the butter and mix with the egg and milk. Mix the yeast, flour, spice, sugar, and milk mixture to a dough in a bowl. Knead for 10 minutes, then put in an oiled bowl and cover with plastic wrap. Leave for 1–2 hours until doubled in size.

3. Butter a 2-lb loaf pan. Melt the chocolate and remaining butter (see page 7). Let cool. Turn the dough onto a floured surface and knead in the raisins. Let stand, covered with a cloth, for 10 minutes. Roll out to a rectangle 13 inches long and as wide as the length of the pan.

4. Spread the cooled chocolate to within ¾ inch of the edges. Scatter with the nuts.

5. Roll up the dough, starting from a short end, and drop it into the pan with the join on top. Cover loosely with oiled plastic wrap and leave in a warm place for 45 minutes or until risen above the rim.

6. Bake in the oven for 45 minutes until deep golden. Turn out, dust with sugar, and let cool.

WHITE CHOCOLATE & CARROT CUPCAKES

These little cakes are perfect for an afternoon treat. Dust them lightly with confectioners' sugar if you don't want the richness of the ganache topping.

SERVES 12

- ½ cup (1 stick) unsalted butter, softened
- ½ cup light brown sugar
- 1¼ cups self-rising flour
- 1 teaspoon baking powder
- ¾ cup ground almonds
- 2 eggs
- 2½ cups grated carrot
- ⅓ cup raisins
- 4 oz white chocolate, chopped
- 1¼ cups heavy cream
- 10 oz dark chocolate, chopped
- White chocolate shavings, to decorate (see page 6)

1. Preheat the oven to 350°F. Line a 12-section muffin pan with paper muffin liners.

2. Beat together the butter, sugar, flour, baking powder, ground almonds, and eggs with an electric hand mixer until pale and creamy.

3. Stir in the carrots, raisins, and chocolate and divide the batter among the paper liners.

4. Bake in the oven for about 20 minutes until risen and firm.

5 In a small saucepan, heat the cream until just bubbling around the edge. Remove from the heat and stir in the chocolate.

6. Turn into a bowl and stir frequently until the chocolate has melted. Cover and chill until the mixture holds its shape before spreading. Spread the cakes with the chocolate ganache and decorate with white chocolate shavings.

CHOCOLATE-ORANGE MADELEINES

SERVES 24

- ¾ cup superfine sugar
- 3 eggs
- ½ teaspoon orange extract
- Pinch of salt
- 1½ cups all-purpose flour, plus extra for dusting
- ½ teaspoon baking powder
- Finely grated zest of 1 orange
- ½ cup (1 stick) butter, melted, plus extra for greasing
- 1–2 tablespoons freshly squeezed orange juice
- Vegetable oil, for greasing
- 10½ oz orange-flavored dark chocolate, broken into pieces

1. In a large bowl, beat together the sugar, eggs, orange extract, and salt for 4–5 minutes, or until doubled in volume. Fold in the flour, baking powder, and orange zest, then add the butter and the orange juice. Cover and place in the refrigerator for at least 2 hours, or preferably overnight.

2. Preheat the oven to 425°F. Grease 24 madeleine molds with melted butter, then dust lightly with flour, tapping out any excess. Remove the batter from the refrigerator, stir gently, and fill each mold about three-quarters full.

3. Bake in the oven for 4 minutes, then reduce the oven temperature to 350°F and bake for 4–5 minutes more, until risen and firm and golden. Immediately remove the madeleines from the molds and transfer to a wire rack to cool.

4. Wash and dry the madeleine molds, then grease lightly with some paper towel dipped in vegetable oil.

5. Melt the chocolate (see page 7). Fill each mold with about 2 teaspoons of the melted chocolate, using the back of the spoon to ensure the mold is well covered.

6. Gently push each cooled madeleine back into a mold and let stand in a cool place for the chocolate to set completely. Use the tip of a knife to gently lever a chocolate-shelled madeleine out of its mold—once set it should come out easily.

TRIPLE CHOCOLATE MUFFINS

SERVES 6
- ⅓ cup dark chocolate chips
- 4 tablespoons (½ stick) unsalted butter
- 2 eggs
- 6 tablespoons superfine sugar
- ¾ cup self-rising flour
- ¼ cup unsweetened cocoa
- 2 tablespoons white chocolate chips

1. Preheat the oven to 350°F.

2. Melt the dark chocolate chips with the butter in a small saucepan over a low heat. Beat together the eggs, sugar, flour, and cocoa in a large bowl. With a metal spatula, fold in the melted chocolate mixture and the white chocolate chips.

3. Spoon the batter into a 6-section muffin pan lined with paper muffin liners and bake in the oven for 12 minutes, until risen and firm to the touch.

4. Transfer the muffins to a wire rack to cool slightly before eating.

WHITE CHOCOLATE CURL CAKES

SERVES 18

- ½ cup plus 2 tablespoons (1¼ sticks) lightly salted butter, softened
- ⅔ cup superfine sugar
- scant 1½ cups self-rising flour
- 3 eggs
- 1 teaspoon vanilla extract
- ⅓ cup white chocolate chips

- 3½ oz chunky piece of white chocolate
- Confectioners' sugar, for dusting

Frosting
- 7 oz white chocolate, chopped
- 5 tablespoons milk
- 1½ cups confectioners' sugar

1. Preheat the oven to 350°F. Line two 12-section mini tart pans with 18 paper cake liners.

2. Put the butter, superfine sugar, flour, eggs, and vanilla extract in a bowl and beat with an electric hand mixer for 1–2 minutes, until pale and creamy. Stir in the chocolate chips. Divide the batter evenly among the paper liners.

3. Bake in the oven for 20 minutes, or until risen and just firm to the touch. Transfer to a wire rack to cool.

4. Pare curls from the piece of chocolate using a vegetable peeler —if the chocolate breaks off in small, brittle shards, try softening it in a microwave oven for a few seconds first, but be careful not to overheat and melt it. Set the chocolate curls aside in a cool place while making the frosting.

5. In a heatproof bowl set over a saucepan of gently simmering water, melt the chocolate with the milk, stirring frequently. Remove from the heat and stir in the sugar until smooth. Use the frosting while still warm. Spread the frosting all over the tops of the cakes, using a small spatula. Pile the chocolate curls onto the cakes and lightly dust with confectioners' sugar.

CHOCOLATE ORANGE CUPCAKES

- - - - - - - -   - - - - - - - - - - - - - - - -

SERVES 12

- ½ cup (1 stick) lightly salted butter, softened
- ½ cup superfine sugar
- 2 eggs
- 1 cup self-rising flour
- ¼ cup unsweetened cocoa
- ½ teaspoon baking powder
- Finely grated zest of 1 orange

- Candied orange peel shavings, to decorate (optional)

Frosting
- 3¼ oz dark chocolate, chopped
- 7 tablespoons (½ stick plus 3 tablespoons) unsalted butter, softened
- 1 cup confectioners' sugar
- 2 tablespoons unsweetened cocoa

1. Preheat the oven to 350°F. Line a 12-section mini tart pan with paper cake liners.

2. Put the lightly salted butter, superfine sugar, eggs, flour, cocoa, baking powder, and orange zest in a bowl and beat with an electric hand mixer for about a minute, until pale and creamy. Divide the batter evenly among the paper liners.

3. Bake in the oven for 20 minutes, or until risen and just firm to the touch. Transfer to a wire rack to cool.

4. Melt the chocolate (see page 7) and let cool. Beat together the unsalted butter, confectioners' sugar, and cocoa in a bowl until smooth and creamy. Stir in the melted chocolate. Pipe or swirl the frosting over the tops of the cakes and decorate with candied orange peel shavings, if liked.

CHOCOLATE ICED FANCIES

SERVES 16

- ½ cup (1 stick) lightly salted butter, softened, plus extra for greasing
- 4 oz dark chocolate, chopped
- ½ cup light brown sugar
- 2 eggs
- ½ cup self-rising flour
- ¼ cup unsweetened cocoa
- ½ cup ground almonds

- 5 tablespoons chocolate hazelnut spread

Frosting
- 7 oz dark chocolate, chopped
- 2 tablespoons corn syrup
- 1 tablespoon lightly salted butter
- 2 oz milk chocolate, chopped

1. Preheat the oven to 325°F. Grease and line a 6-inch square pan with nonstick parchment paper. Grease the paper.

2. Melt the chocolate (see page 7). Beat together the butter and sugar in a bowl until pale and creamy.

3. Gradually beat in the eggs, adding a little flour to prevent the mixture curdling. Stir in the melted chocolate.

4. Sift the flour and cocoa over the bowl. Add the ground almonds and stir in gently. Turn into the prepared pan and level the surface. Bake in the oven for about 20 minutes until risen and just firm to the touch. Transfer to a wire rack to cool.

5. Cut the cake into 16 squares and, using a spatula, spread a little mound of chocolate hazelnut spread on the top of each one.

6. Make the frosting by melting the dark chocolate with the syrup and butter until smooth and glossy (see page 7). Separately melt the milk chocolate. Spoon a little of the dark chocolate mixture over each cake and spread around the sides with a spatula. Using a teaspoon, drizzle lines of milk chocolate over each cake.

FROSTED CHOCOLATE WHOOPIES

SERVES 12-14
- Butter, for greasing
- 1¼ cups self-rising flour
- ¼ teaspoon baking soda
- ¼ cup unsweetened cocoa
- ½ cup superfine sugar
- 2 tablespoons vanilla sugar
- 1 egg
- 3 tablespoons vegetable oil
- 1 tablespoon milk

Filling
- 6 tablespoons cream cheese
- 2 tablespoons confectioners' sugar, sifted
- 1 teaspoon finely grated orange zest
- Few drops orange extract (optional)

1. Preheat the oven to 400°F. Grease a large baking sheet.

2. Put the flour, baking soda, cocoa, and sugars in a bowl. Beat the egg with the vegetable oil and milk and add to the dry ingredients. Beat together to form a thick paste, adding a little more milk if the mixture feels crumbly.

3. Take teaspoonfuls of the mixture and roll into balls, about the size of a cherry, using floured hands. Space well apart on the baking sheet and flatten slightly.

4. Bake in the oven for 12 minutes until the mixture has spread and is pale golden. Transfer to a wire rack to cool.

5. Make the frosting by beating together the cream cheese, confectioners' sugar, orange zest, and orange extract, if using. Use to sandwich the cakes together. Melt the chocolate (see page 7) and spread over the tops of the whoopies.

CHOCOLATE &
PECAN SPIRAL

SERVES 4

Dough
- 2 eggs, beaten
- ¾ cup milk
- 3½ tablespoons (scant ½ stick) unsalted butter, softened
- ½ teaspoon salt
- 4 cups bread flour

- ¼ cup superfine sugar
- 1½ teaspoons instant dried yeast

To finish
- 4 oz dark chocolate, finely chopped
- 1 cup pecan nuts, roughly chopped
- 2 tablespoons superfine sugar
- 1 egg yolk, to glaze

1. Lift the bread pan out of your bread-making machine and fit the blade. Put the dough ingredients in the pan, following the order specified in the manual.

2. Fit the pan into the machine and close the lid. Set to the dough program.

3. At the end of the program, turn the dough out onto a floured surface and roll it to a 11-inch square. Sprinkle over three-quarters of the chocolate and the nuts and all of the sugar. Roll up the dough, then put it into a greased 8-cup loaf pan. Cover loosely with oiled plastic wrap and leave in a warm place for 30 minutes or until the dough reaches just above the top of the pan. Preheat the oven to 400°F.

4. Mix the egg yolk with 1 tablespoon of water and brush it over the dough. Sprinkle over the remaining chocolate and pecan nuts and bake in the oven for 35–40 minutes until the bread is well risen and deep brown and sounds hollow when tapped with the fingertips. Cover with foil after 10 minutes to prevent the nuts from over-browning.

CHOCOLATE CHIP SCONES WITH CITRUS BUTTER

- - - - - - - - - - - - - - - - - - -

These chocolate-studded scones are incredibly easy to make. You needn't even wait for them to cool—they are delicious served warm, split, and buttered.

SERVES 8
- 2 cups self-rising flour
- 1 teaspoon baking powder
- ½ cup (1 stick) unsalted butter, plus extra for greasing
- 3½ oz dark or milk chocolate, finely chopped
- ½ cup confectioners' sugar
- About ½ cup plus 2 tablespoons milk, plus extra for glazing
- Finely grated zest of ½ small orange, plus 2 teaspoons juice

1. Preheat the oven to 425°F. Grease a baking sheet.

2. Sift the flour and baking powder into a bowl. Add 3 tablespoons of the butter, cut into small pieces, and rub in with the fingertips until the mixture resembles fine bread crumbs. Stir in the chocolate, 2 tablespoons of the sugar, and ½ cup of the milk and mix to a soft dough, adding the remaining milk if the dough feels dry.

3. Turn the dough onto a lightly floured surface and roll out to ¾ inch thick. Use a 2½-inch cutter to cut out rounds, re-rolling and cutting out the trimmings as necessary.

4. Transfer to the baking sheet and brush with milk to glaze. Bake in the oven for 12 minutes until well risen and pale golden. Transfer to a wire rack.

5. Meanwhile, beat together the remaining butter and sugar with the orange zest and juice and turn into a small serving dish, ready for spreading over the warm scones.

TRIPLE CHOC & ESPRESSO BROWNIES

Don't be fooled by the white chocolate layer and the milk chocolate chips; the rich chocolate and strong espresso flavors make this an extremely grown-up brownie!

SERVES 16

- 1 cup (2 sticks) butter, plus extra for greasing
- 8 oz dark chocolate, broken into pieces
- 3 eggs
- 2 tablespoons strong espresso-style coffee
- ⅔ cup superfine sugar
- ½ cup packed dark brown sugar
- ⅔ cup self-rising flour
- Pinch of salt
- Generous ½ cup milk chocolate chips
- ½ cup coarsely grated white chocolate

1. Preheat the oven to 400°F. Grease a 13 x 9-inch brownie pan and line the bottom with parchment paper.

2. In a small, heavy-bottom saucepan, slowly melt the butter with the dark chocolate, stir until smooth, then set aside to cool.

3. In a large bowl, beat the eggs with the espresso and sugars, followed by the melted chocolate. Add the flour and salt and mix until well combined, then stir in the milk chocolate chips.

4. Pour half the brownie mixture into the prepared pan, then scatter over the grated white chocolate, pressing down gently with fingertips. Cover with the remaining brownie mixture and bake in the oven for 20–25 minutes. The brownie should rise but still be slightly soft in the center. Let cool for at least 10 minutes before cutting into squares. Serve slightly warm, or cool completely and store in an airtight container between layers of wax paper.

TIP

- Try this recipe with other flavored chocolates, such as dark mint or praline chocolate. You could also make a layer with chopped nuts or raisins.

PRUNE & ORANGE SLICES

Wrap up these rich, dark chocolate slices to make a delightful gift, or serve with strong coffee as an after-dinner treat, or when cravings demand!

SERVES 24

- ¾ cup plus 2 tablespoons (1¾ sticks) butter
- 7 oz orange-flavored dark chocolate, broken into pieces
- 5½ oz milk chocolate, broken into pieces
- 7 oz shortbread cookies
- Finely grated zest of 1 orange
- 1 cup chopped prunes
- 2 tablespoons chopped candied orange peel
- ½ cup white chocolate chips

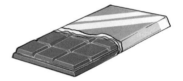

1. Line a 13 x 9-inch baking pan with a large sheet of plastic wrap, with enough extra to fold over the top.

2. In a medium, heavy-bottom saucepan over low heat, slowly melt the butter with the dark chocolate and milk chocolate, stir until smooth, then set aside to cool.

3. Place the shortbread cookies in a plastic bag and tap with a rolling pin to break up into pieces.

4. Stir the orange zest, prunes, candied peel, and cookie pieces into the melted chocolate and stir well until thoroughly coated. Stir in the white chocolate chips.

5. Turn the mixture into the prepared pan and press down gently into the pan to cover the bottom but not so much that it is completely smooth. Cover the surface with the plastic wrap and place in the refrigerator for at least an hour, or until cold and hardened.

6. Turn out onto a chopping board and cut into slices. Store in an airtight container between layers of wax paper.

CHERRY & CHOCOLATE NUT SLICES

Although macadamia nuts taste wonderful alongside the cherries and chocolate, you can substitute them with hazelnuts, which will work equally well.

SERVES 9

- ½ cup plus 1 tablespoon (1 stick plus 1 tablespoon) butter, plus extra for greasing
- 7 oz dark chocolate, broken into pieces
- ½ cup dark corn syrup
- 12 oz gingersnap cookies
- ⅔ cup candied cherries, halved
- ⅔ cup roughly chopped, toasted macadamia nuts

1. Grease an 8-inch square, loose-bottom cake pan and line the bottom with parchment paper.

2. In a small, heavy-bottom saucepan over low heat, melt the butter with the chocolate and corn syrup, stir until smooth, then set aside.

3. Place half the gingersnap cookies in a food processor and process to fine crumbs. Roughly chop the remaining cookies, then add both to the melted chocolate mixture, along with the cherries and nuts. Mix until well combined.

4. Spoon the chocolate mixture into the prepared pan and let set in the refrigerator for 2 hours.

5. Remove from the pan, peel off the parchment paper, and cut into slices.

REALLY MOIST CHOCOLATE SLICE

Plenty of almonds and butter give this moist cake a rich flavor. For an everyday version, dust the cake with confectioners' sugar instead of filling and covering it with chocolate cream.

SERVES 12-14

- 8 oz dark chocolate, broken into pieces
- 1 cup (2 sticks) unsalted butter, melted, plus extra for greasing
- 5 eggs
- ¼ cup light brown sugar
- 1 cup self-rising flour
- ¾ cup ground almonds

Chocolate cream
- ½ cup plus 2 tablespoons heavy cream
- 5 oz dark chocolate, chopped

1. Preheat the oven to 325°F. Grease and line a 9-inch square cake pan.

2. Melt the chocolate (see page 7) and then stir in the butter.

3. Beat together the eggs and sugar until slightly thickened. Sift the flour over the mixture, then add the almonds and chocolate mixture and fold in until evenly combined. Turn into the prepared pan and bake in the oven for about 35 minutes until just firm. Transfer to a wire rack to cool.

4. Meanwhile, make the chocolate cream. Heat the cream in a saucepan until almost boiling. Remove the pan from the heat and add the chocolate. Leave until the chocolate has melted, then stir until smooth. Transfer to a bowl and let cool until thickened.

5. Slice off the top of the cake if it has risen in the center. Halve the cake horizontally and sandwich the halves with one-third of the chocolate cream. Spread the remainder over the top and sides of the cake, swirling it decoratively with a spatula.

WHITE CHOCOLATE BISCOTTI

These gorgeous cookies are baked in one piece, then sliced and re-baked to crisp them up. Serve the Italian way dunked into dessert wine or with some creamy hot chocolate.

SERVES 24

- 10 oz white chocolate
- 2 tablespoons (¼ stick) unsalted butter, softened, plus extra for greasing
- Scant 2 cups self-rising flour
- ¼ cup light brown sugar
- 2 eggs
- 1 teaspoon vanilla extract
- Scant 1 cup pecan nuts, roughly chopped
- Confectioners' sugar, for dusting

1. Preheat the oven to 375°F. Lightly grease a large baking sheet.

2. Chop one-third of the chocolate into small pieces. Break up the remainder and melt it with the butter (see page 7). Let cool. Sift the flour into a mixing bowl and stir in the sugar, eggs, vanilla extract, nuts, and melted chocolate mixture.

3. Add the chopped chocolate and mix to a dough. Tip the mixture onto a lightly floured surface and halve the dough.

4. Shape each half into a log about 10 inches long and flatten to a depth of ¾ inch. Space well apart on the baking sheet and bake in the oven for 18–20 minutes until risen, golden, and firm. Remove from the oven and reduce the temperature to 325°F.

5. Leave the cookie logs to cool for 20 minutes, then use a serrated knife to slice each length into slices ¾ inch thick. Space them slightly apart on the baking sheet and bake for an additional 15 minutes. Dust with confectioners' sugar and transfer to a wire rack to cool.

THYME, ORANGE & CHOCOLATE SHORTBREAD

Buttery homemade shortbread is always a real treat, and the subtle additions in this recipe make it even more irresistible.

SERVES 25

- 1 tablespoon chopped thyme
- ¼ cup superfine sugar
- 5 oz milk or white chocolate, broken into pieces
- 2 cups all-purpose flour
- ¾ cup rice flour
- Finely grated zest of 1 orange
- ¾ cup plus 2 tablespoons (1¾ sticks) lightly salted butter, diced, plus extra for greasing

1. Preheat the oven to 350°F. Grease 2 baking sheets.

2. Reserve 1 teaspoon of the chopped thyme. Sprinkle the remainder over 2 tablespoons of the sugar on a chopping board and press the thyme into the sugar with the side of a knife. Melt the chocolate (see page 7).

3. Sift the flour and rice flour into a mixing bowl. Add the reserved thyme, orange zest, and butter and rub in with the fingertips until the mixture resembles coarse bread crumbs.

4. Stir in the remaining sugar and the melted chocolate and mix with a round-bladed knife until the mixture starts to form a dough. Use your hands to bring the mixture together and turn it onto the work surface.

5. Shape into a thick log, about 12 inches long. Roll up in wax paper and chill for 1 hour.

6. Roll the log in the herb sugar. Cut across into thick slices and space slightly apart on the baking sheet. Bake in the oven for about 20 minutes until beginning to turn pale golden. Transfer to a wire rack to cool.

CHOCOLATE PEANUT CARAMELS

The combination of salty peanuts and smooth, sweet chocolate always works well in baking. This moreish mixture is very rich, so cut it into small squares.

SERVES ABOUT 25
- 1 quantity Chocolate Pastry (see page 115)
- ½ cup salted peanuts
- ¾ cup plus 2 tablespoons golden baker's sugar (or superfine)
- ¾ cup plus 2 tablespoons heavy cream
- 4 tablespoons (½ stick) unsalted butter, plus extra for greasing
- 4 oz dark chocolate, chopped

1. Preheat the oven to 350°F. Grease the bottom of a shallow 9-inch square baking pan.

2. Roll out the pastry on a lightly floured surface and pack it into the prepared pan, pressing it down in an even layer. Bake in the oven for 20 minutes until slightly darker in color.

3. Blend the peanuts in a food processor or blender until they are ground into small pieces. Put the sugar in a small heavy-bottom saucepan with 6 tablespoons water. Heat gently until the sugar dissolves, then bring to a boil and boil rapidly for about 5 minutes until the syrup has turned deep golden. Dip the bottom of the pan straight into cold water to prevent further cooking.

4. Add ½ cup of the cream and the butter and stir over a gentle heat until smooth. Stir in the nuts and let thicken for about 15 minutes. Turn the mixture into the pastry-lined pan, spreading it to the edges.

5. Heat the remaining cream in a small pan until almost boiling. Remove from the heat and stir in the chocolate. Leave until melted, stirring frequently until smooth. Tip out over the caramel and spread in an even layer. Chill for at least 2 hours until firm. Serve cut into small squares.

CHOCOLATE OATY WEDGES

- - - - - - - - - - - - - - - - - - - -

SERVES 12
- ½ cup (1 stick) margarine, plus extra for greasing
- 4 tablespoons corn syrup
- ¼ cup raw sugar
- 2 cups rolled oats
- ½ teaspoon finely grated orange zest (optional)

Topping
- 3 oz dark chocolate, broken into pieces
- 3 tablespoons shredded coconut

1. Preheat the oven to 350°F. Grease an 8-inch round shallow cake pan.

2. Put the margarine, corn syrup, and sugar in a large saucepan and heat gently until melted. Remove from the heat.

3. Stir in the oats and orange zest, if using, and mix well. Turn into the prepared pan and spread out evenly.

4. Bake in the oven for 15 minutes until lightly golden.

5. Meanwhile, prepare the topping. Melt the chocolate (see page 7). Spread the melted chocolate over the hot baked mixture in the pan and sprinkle with shredded coconut. Cut into 12 wedges and let cool in the pan for 1 hour. Store in an airtight container.

DOUBLE CHOC-CHIP COOKIES

These cookies are the ultimate chocolate experience—double the chocolate, double the taste!

SERVES 14

- ¾ cup (1½ sticks) butter, plus extra for greasing
- ⅔ cup superfine sugar
- 1 egg, beaten
- 1–2 teaspoons vanilla extract
- 1¾ cups all-purpose flour
- 1 teaspoon baking powder
- 2 oz good-quality dark chocolate, broken into pieces
- 2 oz good-quality white chocolate, broken into pieces

1. Preheat the oven to 350°F. Lightly grease a large baking sheet.

2. Beat together the butter and sugar until pale and creamy. Beat in the egg and vanilla extract. Sift the flour and baking powder together and beat into the mixture. Add the chocolate and stir until mixed.

3. Heap 5–6 rounded tablespoons of the cookie mixture onto the baking sheet at a time, leaving plenty of space between them as the cookies will almost double in size. Bake in the oven for 12–15 minutes until golden.

4. Let cool on the baking sheet for 2–3 minutes, then transfer to a wire rack to cool completely. Cookies can be stored in an airtight container for up to 1 week.

CLASSIC CHOCOLATE TRUFFLES P122

SWEET TREATS

CHOCOLATE BRIOCHE SANDWICH

SERVES 1
- 2 slices brioche
- 1 tablespoon ready-made chocolate spread
- 1 tablespoon (⅛ stick) butter, softened
- 2 teaspoons light brown sugar

1. Spread 1 slice of brioche with chocolate spread, then top with the other slice.

2. Butter the outsides of the chocolate sandwich and sprinkle with the sugar.

3. Heat a griddle, skillet, or sandwich maker, and cook the chocolate brioche for 3 minutes, turning as needed.

GOOEY CHOCOLATE NUT BREAD

SERVES 8-10

Dough
- 1 large egg, beaten
- ½ cup plus 2 tablespoons milk
- 2 teaspoons vanilla bean paste
- 6 tablespoons (¾ stick) unsalted butter, softened, plus extra for greasing
- ¼ teaspoon salt
- 3 cups bread flour
- ½ cup ground hazelnuts
- ¼ cup superfine sugar

- 1¼ teaspoons instant dried yeast

To finish
- 1 cup chocolate hazelnut spread
- ⅔ cup hazelnuts, roughly chopped, plus ¼ cup to decorate
- Beaten egg, to glaze
- 2 oz dark chocolate, chopped
- Unsweetened cocoa and confectioners' sugar, for dusting

1. Grease an 8-inch loose-bottom round cake pan.

2. Lift the bread pan out of your bread-making machine and fit the blade. Put the dough ingredients in the pan, following the order specified in the manual. Add the ground hazelnuts with the flour. Fit the pan into the machine and close the lid. Set to the dough program.

3. At the end of the program, turn the dough out onto a floured surface. Roll one-third of the dough to a 10½-inch round. Place it in the cake pan so it comes about 1¼ inches up the sides to make a shell.

4. Dot one-third of the chocolate spread over the bottom and scatter with one-third of the nuts. Divide the remaining dough into three pieces and roll each to an 8-inch round. Place one layer in the pan and dot with another third of chocolate spread and nuts. Continue to layer, finishing with a dough round.

5. Brush the top of the dough with beaten egg. Press the chopped chocolate and ¼ cup hazelnuts into the dough. Cover loosely with oiled plastic wrap and allow to rise in a warm place for 45–60 minutes or until about half the size again. Preheat the oven to 400°F.

6. Bake in the oven for 50 minutes. Cover it with foil if the top starts to over-brown. Transfer to a wire rack to cool. Serve dusted with cocoa and confectioners' sugar.

CHOC CINNAMON FRENCH TOAST

SERVES 2

- 2 eggs, lightly beaten
- 2 thick slices seeded brown bread, cut in half
- 1 tablespoon (⅛ stick) butter
- 2 tablespoons golden baker's sugar (or superfine)
- 2 teaspoons unsweetened cocoa
- ½ teaspoon ground cinnamon

1. Place the eggs in a shallow dish. Press the bread into the egg mixture, turning to coat well.

2. Melt the butter in a heavy-bottom skillet and add the eggy bread. Cook for 3 minutes, turning as needed.

3. Mix the sugar, cocoa, and cinnamon on a plate and place the hot French toast on top, turning as needed to coat. Serve immediately.

CHOCOLATE, DATE & ALMOND PANINI

SERVES 4
- 3 tablespoons whole blanched almonds
- 2 tablespoons confectioners' sugar
- ¾ cup finely grated white chocolate
- 8 soft dates, pitted and chopped
- ¼ cup slivered almonds, lightly toasted
- 8 slices brioche, buttered on both sides
- ¼ cup heavy cream, whipped

1. Preheat the oven to 350°F.

2. Put the blanched almonds in a colander and sprinkle with a little cold water. Shake off any excess water and place the almonds on a nonstick baking sheet. Sift the confectioners' sugar over the top and bake in the oven for about 20 minutes until they have crystallized.

3. Remove the almonds from the oven and set aside to cool, then put them in a plastic bag and tap lightly with a rolling pin until they are crushed but not powdery.

4. Mix together the grated chocolate, dates, and toasted almonds. Spoon the mixture onto four slices of the buttered brioche and top with the remaining slices to make four sandwiches.

5. Heat a griddle over a medium heat and cook the brioche sandwiches for 3–4 minutes. Turn them over and cook the other side for another 3–4 minutes to make a panini.

6. Cut the panini in half diagonally and serve immediately with whipped cream and sprinkled with crushed almonds.

CHOCOLATE SWIRL TART

This tart is so easy to make that it will quickly become a firm favorite. The amaretti cookies add a delicious almond flavor.

SERVES 6-8

Crumb shell
- 8 graham crackers
- 2 oz amaretti cookies
- 6 tablespoons (¾ stick) butter, plus extra for greasing

Filling
- 7 oz dark chocolate
- 1 cup heavy cream

1. Put the graham crackers and cookies in a plastic bag and crush them with a rolling pin. Melt the butter in a saucepan and stir in the cookie crumbs. Press the mixture into a greased 9-inch pie dish. Chill until firm.

2. Put the chocolate in a heatproof bowl over a pan of hot water. Stir gently until melted. Cover a rolling pin with foil and brush lightly with oil. Drizzle a little chocolate onto the rolling pin in zigzag lines, about 1 inch long. Chill until set.

3. Beat the cream until stiff and fold into the remaining melted chocolate. Spoon into the crumb shell and chill for 2 hours until set.

4. Just before serving, carefully peel the chocolate decorations from the foil and arrange them in the center of the tart.

WHITE CHOCOLATE CHERRY TART

- -

The perfect marriage of chocolate and cherries is both traditional and highly successful. Cinnamon and chocolate is another favorite partnership.

SERVES 6-8

Pastry
- 1½ cups all-purpose flour
- ½ teaspoon ground cinnamon
- ½ cup (1 stick) unsalted butter, diced
- 2 tablespoons superfine sugar
- 2–3 tablespoons ice water

Filling
- 2 eggs
- 3 tablespoons superfine sugar
- 5 oz white chocolate, finely chopped
- 1¼ cups heavy cream
- 2 cups fresh black or red cherries, pitted, or 2 x 14 oz cans pitted black or red cherries, drained
- Ground cinnamon, for dusting

1. Preheat the oven to 350°F.

2. Make the pastry. Sift the flour and cinnamon into a bowl, add the butter and rub in with the fingertips. Add the sugar and just enough water to mix to a firm dough. Roll out the dough and line a 9-inch loose-bottom tart pan. Chill for 30 minutes, then bake blind in the oven for 10 minutes (see page 139). Remove the paper and pie weights or foil and return to the oven for an additional 5 minutes.

3. Beat together the eggs and sugar. Heat the chocolate and cream in a small bowl over hot water until the chocolate has melted. Pour over the egg mixture, stirring constantly.

4. Arrange the cherries in the tart shell. Pour the chocolate mixture over the cherries.

5. Bake in the oven for about 45 minutes until the chocolate cream is set. Dust with cinnamon and serve warm.

WHITE CHOCOLATE & CRANBERRY TARTS

SERVES 6

- 2 cups frozen cranberries
- ¼ cup golden baker's sugar (or superfine)
- 4 tablespoons crème de cassis
- 7 oz creamy vanilla white chocolate
- 1¼ cups fat-free fromage frais or yogurt
- 1 teaspoon vanilla bean paste
- 2 tablespoons cranberry jelly
- 6 ready-made all-butter tart shells

1. Gently heat the cranberries, sugar, and crème de cassis in a saucepan for a few minutes until the cranberries are just softened. Strain the cranberries and set aside to cool, reserving the juice.

2. Melt the white chocolate (see page 7). Stir in the fromage frais and vanilla bean paste and beat together well. Cover and chill.

3. Add the cranberry jelly to the reserved cranberry juice in the pan. Heat gently to melt the jelly and then stir to combine.

4. Spoon the vanilla and white chocolate mixture into the tart shells 1–2 hours before serving. Top with the cranberries and spoon the cranberry syrup over to glaze. Chill until needed.

CHOCOLATE VELVET PIE

This chocolate shortbread is an interesting variation on traditional plain shortbread. Swirls of whipped heavy cream would make a decadent finishing touch.

SERVES 10

Shortbread
- ½ cup (1 stick) unsalted butter, diced
- 1½ cups all-purpose flour
- 2 teaspoons unsweetened cocoa
- 2 tablespoons superfine sugar

Filling
- 4 teaspoons powdered gelatin
- 3 tablespoons cold water
- ½ cup superfine sugar

- 3 egg yolks
- 1 tablespoon cornstarch
- 2½ cups milk
- 2 tablespoons finely ground espresso powder
- 2 oz dark chocolate, broken into pieces
- Chocolate shavings, to decorate (see page 9)

1. Preheat the oven to 350°F.

2. Rub the butter into the sifted flour and cocoa, add the sugar, and mix to a dough. Press evenly over the bottom and sides of a deep 8-inch fluted tart pan. Bake in the oven for 20 minutes, then let cool.

3. Soak the gelatin in the water. Whisk the sugar, egg yolks, cornstarch, and 2 tablespoons of the milk. Bring the rest of the milk to a boil with the coffee powder. Whisk it into the egg mixture.

4. Return the mixture to the saucepan and heat gently, stirring until it thickens. Remove from the heat and beat in the gelatin until dissolved. Add the chocolate and stir until it has melted. Cool slightly, then pour the mixture into the tart shell. Chill for several hours.

5. Transfer the pie to a plate and scatter generously with chocolate shavings.

WHITE CHOCOLATE & LAVENDER CUPS

SERVES 16

- 4 oz white chocolate, chopped
- 16 small amaretti cookies
- 4 tablespoons almond-flavored liqueur or orange juice
- 3 lavender flowers, plus extra to decorate
- Finely grated zest of ½ orange
- 3 tablespoons superfine sugar
- 1¼ cups heavy cream
- White chocolate shavings, to decorate (see page 9)

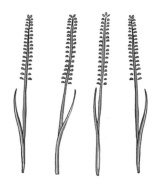

1. Melt the chocolate (see page 7). Place a teaspoonful into each of 16 mini silicone cupcake molds and spread up the sides with the back of the teaspoon until evenly coated. Invert onto a baking sheet lined with nonstick parchment paper. Chill for at least 1 hour or until set.

2. Carefully peel away the silicone cups and place the chocolate cups upright. Place an amaretti cookie in each chocolate cup and drizzle with the liqueur or orange juice.

3. Pull the lavender flowers from the stalks and put in a pestle with the orange zest and sugar. Pound the ingredients to bruise and mingle the flavors together.

4. Turn into a bowl with the cream and beat until the cream is only just holding its shape. Spoon into the cups and decorate with lavender flowers and white chocolate shavings.

5. Serve immediately or chill for up to 6 hours.

WHITE CHOCOLATE & RASPBERRY PUFFS

SERVES 6
- 12 oz puff pastry (thawed if frozen)
- 1¼ cups raspberries
- Confectioners' sugar, for dusting

White chocolate cream
- ¾ cup plus 2 tablespoons light cream
- ½ vanilla bean
- 7 oz white chocolate, chopped

1. Preheat the oven to 400°F.

2. Roll out the pastry on a lightly floured surface until it forms a rectangle 1/8 inch thick. Cut the pastry into six rectangles, each 3 x 5 inches, and put them on a baking sheet. Chill for 30 minutes. Bake in the oven for 15 minutes or until the pastry is puffed and golden. Transfer to a wire rack to cool.

3. Make the chocolate cream. Put the cream and vanilla bean in a heavy-bottom saucepan and heat gently until it reaches boiling point. Remove from the heat and scrape the seeds from the vanilla bean into the cream (discard the pod). Immediately stir in the chocolate and continue stirring until it has melted. Let cool, chill for 1 hour until firm, and then whisk until stiff.

4. Split the pastries in half crosswise and fill each with white chocolate cream and raspberries. Serve dusted with confectioners' sugar.

SPICED CHOCOLATE PASTRIES

- -

Oozing with molten chocolate, these unusual pastries are delicious with tea or freshly brewed coffee.

SERVES 9

- 8 oz puff pastry, thawed if frozen
- Flour, for dusting
- 1 egg yolk
- 2 tablespoons milk
- 18 squares dark chocolate
- 1 teaspoon grated orange zest
- Pinch of ground star anise
- Butter, for greasing

1. Preheat the oven to 400°F. Grease a baking sheet.

2. Roll out the pastry thinly on a lightly floured surface and trim to form a 9-inch square. Cut into thirds crosswise and lengthwise to form nine squares.

3. Beat the egg yolk and milk to make a glaze and brush a little around the edges of each pastry square. Place two squares of chocolate, a little orange zest, and a touch of star anise on each one. Fold diagonally in half and press the edges together to seal.

4. Place the pastries on the prepared baking sheet and bake in the oven for 12 minutes, until risen and golden. Let cool on a wire rack for a few minutes before serving.

ESPRESSO TART WITH CHOCOLATE PASTRY

SERVES 8

Pastry
- 1¾ cups flour
- 6 tablespoons good-quality unsweetened cocoa
- ¼ cup golden baker's sugar (or superfine)
- ½ cup plus 2 tablespoons (1¼ sticks) butter, diced
- 1 large egg, beaten
- 2–3 tablespoons iced water

Filling
- 1¾ cups heavy cream
- 3 eggs
- ½ cup golden baker's sugar (or superfine)
- 2 tablespoons instant espresso coffee powder
- 1 oz dark chocolate, grated
- Grated dark chocolate, to decorate

1. Preheat the oven to 350°F.

2. Make the pastry. Sift the flour and cocoa into a bowl. Add the sugar and butter and mix with the fingertips until the mixture resembles bread crumbs. Add the egg and just enough water to make a firm dough. Roll out the pastry and line a 9-inch tart pan. Chill for 30 minutes, then trim the edges.

3. Bake the pastry shell blind in the oven for 15 minutes (see page 139). Remove the pie weights and paper or foil and return the tart to the oven for an additional 10 minutes.

4. Heat the cream until it boils. Whisk the eggs, sugar, and coffee powder, then pour the hot cream over them, stirring continually. Pour the mixture through a fine sieve and then into the tart shell.

5. Bake in the oven for 30–35 minutes or until set. Remove from the oven and sprinkle with grated dark chocolate. Let cool before serving.

CHOCOLATE MOCHA MERINGUES

SERVES 8

- 6 egg whites
- 1⅔ cups light brown sugar
- 2 teaspoons vanilla extract
- 2 tablespoons cornstarch
- 1 tablespoon instant espresso coffee powder
- 1 tablespoon white wine vinegar
- 3 oz dark chocolate, broken into pieces
- 8 tablespoons whole milk yogurt
- 8 teaspoons honey
- 8 figs

1. Preheat the oven to 300°F.

2. Whisk the egg whites in a grease-free bowl until they are stiff. (Test if they are ready by upturning the bowl. If the egg whites slide around, they need to be whisked a little more; if they stay in place, they are ready.)

3. Whisk in the sugar 1 tablespoon at a time until it is all mixed in. Mix together the vanilla extract, cornstarch, coffee powder, and vinegar and fold into the meringue along with the chocolate pieces.

4. Line a baking sheet with nonstick parchment paper. Dollop eight large spoonfuls of meringue onto the sheet. Bake in the oven for 1 hour. Cool.

5. Serve the meringues on individual plates, each with a spoonful of yogurt and a drizzle of honey. Cut a cross in the top of each fig and gently squeeze it at the bottom to open it up. Put one fig on each plate to finish.

CHOCOLATE DATES WITH PISTACHIOS

These are lovely with after-dinner coffee or as a present for someone who isn't too keen on the sweeter chocolate treats.

MAKES 18
- ¼ cup shelled pistachio nuts
- 2 tablespoons confectioners' sugar
- 1 tablespoon superfine sugar
- 1 tablespoon orange liqueur
- 18 Medjool dates
- 3½ oz dark or orange-flavored dark chocolate, broken into pieces

1. Put the pistachios in a small bowl and cover with boiling water. Leave for 1 minute, then drain. Rub firmly between several thicknesses of paper towel to remove the skins.

2. Put the pistachios in a food processor and blend until fairly finely ground. Add the sugars and liqueur and blend to a thick paste. Turn onto the work surface and shape into a thin log. Cut into 18 evenly sized pieces.

3. Cut a slit across the top of each date and remove the pit. Tuck a piece of the pistachio paste in the center.

4. Melt the chocolate in a small bowl (see page 7). Half-dip the stuffed dates in the chocolate and transfer to a sheet of nonstick parchment paper. Leave to set in a very cool place or in the refrigerator for about 1 hour.

ROCKY ROADS

MAKES ABOUT 30

- 4 oz dark or milk chocolate, broken into pieces
- 2 tablespoons (¼ stick) unsalted butter
- 2 tablespoons unsalted peanuts
- 3 tablespoons raisins
- 1 cup mini marshmallows (or ordinary marshmallows, chopped)
- 2 oz white chocolate, broken into pieces
- ½ cup slivered almonds, toasted

1. Melt the dark or milk chocolate with the butter (see page 7).

2. Stir lightly, then add the peanuts, raisins, and marshmallows, and stir gently until coated.

3. Turn out onto a sheet of wax paper and wrap the paper around the mixture, pressing it into a 1½-inch thick roll. Chill until firm.

4. Melt the broken white chocolate.

5. Unwrap the roll. Scatter the almonds over a clean sheet of wax paper. Working quickly, spread the chocolate roll with the white chocolate, then coat in the slivered almonds.

6. Chill until firm and serve cut into thin slices.

CHOCOLATE TOFFEE

A sticky toothsome treat! Successful toffee-making is all about the sugar reaching the correct temperature. The easiest way to guarantee success is to use a candy thermometer.

MAKES ABOUT 36 PIECES

- 2 cups raw sugar
- 1 cup plus 2 tablespoons (2¼ sticks) butter
- ¾ cup corn syrup
- ¼ cup unsweetened cocoa

1. Line an 8-inch square cake pan with nonstick parchment paper.

2. Place all the ingredients in a large, heavy-bottom saucepan and cook slowly, stirring, until the sugar has dissolved.

3. Turn the heat up and bring to a boil until the temperature reaches hard-ball stage (248°F) on a candy thermometer. If you don't have a thermometer, drop a little bit of the mixture into a bowl of cold water and if it hardens immediately it is ready.

4. Pour the mixture into the prepared pan and leave until cold and hard. Cut into pieces.

TIP

- Don't be afraid to keep testing the toffee with your candy thermometer to make sure you reach hard-ball stage.

WHITE CHOCOLATE MINT TRUFFLES

Smooth white chocolate truffles lightly flavored with crushed peppermints are perfect for an after-dinner candy. You could roll the truffles in grated white chocolate instead of the confectioners' sugar.

MAKES 20

- ½ cup heavy cream
- 5 oz white chocolate, broken into pieces
- 1 oz strong, hard, white peppermints
- ⅓ cup confectioners' sugar

1. Pour the cream into a heavy-bottom saucepan and add the chocolate. Heat gently, stirring occasionally, for 4–5 minutes until the chocolate has melted. Let cool.

2. Whisk the cream mixture until thick, then chill in the refrigerator for 3–4 hours.

3. Put the peppermints into a plastic bag, crush with a rolling pin, then stir into the chilled cream mixture. Drop teaspoons of the soft mixture onto a plate and chill for 1 hour or freeze for 30 minutes until firm.

4. Sprinkle the confectioners' sugar on another plate, then roll the truffles in the sugar to form neat balls. Pack into a small box lined with wax paper and dust with the remaining sugar. Chill for at least 2 hours before serving. The truffles can be stored in the refrigerator for up to 4 days.

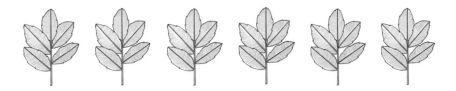

CLASSIC CHOCOLATE TRUFFLES

These are as good as the absolute best you can buy. They are meltingly smooth and creamy and have the added advantage that you can use your favorite liqueur.

MAKES 6

- ½ cup plus 2 tablespoons heavy cream
- 8 oz dark chocolate, finely chopped
- 2 tablespoons (¼ stick) unsalted butter, diced
- 2 tablespoons liqueur (e.g. brandy, rum, Cointreau, or coffee liqueur)
- Unsweetened cocoa, for dusting

1. Bring the cream just to a boil in a small saucepan. Remove from the heat and tip in the chocolate and butter. Leave until melted, stirring several times until smooth.

2. Turn into a bowl and add the chosen liqueur. Chill for several hours or overnight until firm.

3. Sprinkle plenty of unsweetened cocoa on a large plate. Take a teaspoonful of the chocolate mixture, roll it lightly in the palm of your hand, and coat the ball in the cocoa. For more rugged, textured-looking truffles, don't roll them, just sprinkle the spoonfuls of chocolate with the cocoa powder.

4. Arrange the truffles in individual paper cups or pile them on a serving dish. Store in a very cool place or in the refrigerator for up to 2 days before serving.

> **TIP**
>
> • For a different flavor, add 3 pieces of stem ginger, finely chopped, or 1 tablespoon instant espresso powder, dissolved in 1 tablespoon boiling water, to the basic mixture before chilling.

CREAMY MINT-CHOC FUDGE

There is no thermometer or sugar boiling to worry about with this creamy, melt-in-the-mouth fudge recipe. Use the very best chocolate for rich and delicious results.

MAKES 25 PIECES

- 1½ oz strong peppermints
- 1 lb dark chocolate, chopped
- 13 oz can sweetened condensed milk
- 2 oz milk or white chocolate

1. Put the peppermints in a plastic bag and crush with a rolling pin until broken into small pieces. Continue to roll and flatten the mints until ground to a powder. Line a shallow 7-inch square baking pan with nonstick parchment paper.

2. Put the dark chocolate and condensed milk in a heatproof bowl over a pan of gently simmering water. Leave until melted, stirring frequently. Stir in the ground peppermints.

3. Beat the mixture until the ingredients are combined and turn it into the prepared pan, spreading it into the corners. Level the surface and let cool. Chill for at least 2 hours.

4. Lift the fudge out of the pan and peel away the paper from around the sides. Melt the milk or white chocolate (see page 7) and put it in a paper pastry bag. Snip off the tip and scribble lines of chocolate over the fudge. Cut into ¾-inch squares and transfer to a serving plate.

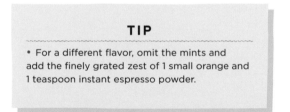

TIP

- For a different flavor, omit the mints and add the finely grated zest of 1 small orange and 1 teaspoon instant espresso powder.

TOFFEE & CHOCOLATE POPCORN

SERVES 4
- ¼ cup popping corn
- 1 cup (2 sticks) butter
- 1 cup light brown sugar
- 2 tablespoons unsweetened cocoa

1. Microwave the popping corn in a large bowl with a lid on high (900 watts) for 4 minutes. Alternatively, cook in a large saucepan with a lid on the stovetop, on a medium heat, for a few minutes until popping.

2. Meanwhile, gently heat the butter, brown sugar, and cocoa in a saucepan until the sugar has dissolved and the butter has melted.

3. Stir the warm popcorn into the mixture and serve.

CINNAMON
LASSI

A drink fit for almost any time of day, from a leisurely breakfast through to a late-afternoon cooler. Any extra keeps well in the refrigerator overnight.

SERVES 2

- ¾ cup plus 2 tablespoons milk
- ½ teaspoon ground cinnamon
- 3 oz dark chocolate, broken into pieces
- ¾ cup plain yogurt
- 3 tablespoons vanilla syrup
- 2 long cinnamon sticks
- Chocolate curls, to decorate (see page 9)

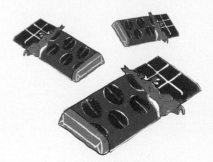

1. Put half the milk in a small saucepan with the cinnamon. Bring just to a boil, then remove it from the heat and stir in the chocolate. Leave until melted, stirring frequently.

2. Stir in the remaining milk, the yogurt, and the vanilla syrup and whisk until frothy with either a balloon or immersion whisk.

3. Pour into glasses and add a cinnamon stick to each. Serve scattered with chocolate curls.

CHOCOLATE MARTINIS

- -

If you have a cocktail shaker, use it to mix the drink with plenty of crushed ice. If not, make it a couple of hours in advance so that it has time to chill.

SERVES 4
- Plenty of unsweetened cocoa, for dusting
- Scant ½ cup gin, plus 1 tablespoon
- 1½ oz dark chocolate, broken into pieces
- ¾ cup plus 2 tablespoons dry vermouth

1. Sprinkle plenty of cocoa on a plate. Use your finger to moisten the rims of four cocktail glasses with the tablespoon of gin. Immediately dip each rim in the cocoa powder to coat in a thin band.

2. Melt the chocolate (see page 7) with the remaining gin, stirring frequently, until the mixture is smooth. Stir in the vermouth.

3. Shake the mixture in a cocktail shaker with ice, or chill for at least 2 hours, before serving.

SUBLIME HOT CHOCOLATE

Proper hot chocolate is always made with a pure blend of good-quality chocolate and milk. The creamy topping is a delicious indulgence but not absolutely vital.

SERVES 2
- 3½ oz dark chocolate, broken into pieces
- 1½ cups milk
- Scant ½ cup whipping cream, lightly whipped
- Grated chocolate, to sprinkle

1. Melt the chocolate (see page 7). Heat the milk in a small saucepan until hot but not boiling. Stir a little of the hot milk into the melted chocolate, scraping up the chocolate from around the sides of the bowl, then pour the chocolate milk into the milk pan.

2. Whisk together and pour into large mugs or heatproof glasses. Spoon over the cream and sprinkle with grated chocolate.

TIP

- For a sweeter flavor, use a good-quality milk chocolate.

IRISH CHOCOLATE COFFEE

Smooth, comforting, and with a warming smack of whiskey, this creamy chocolate coffee is the perfect tipple to relax with.

SERVES 2
- I small orange
- I tablespoon superfine sugar
- I oz dark chocolate, chopped
- 2 tablespoons Irish whiskey
- 1¼ cups freshly made strong black coffee
- Scant ½ cup whipping cream

1. Pare 2 long strips of orange zest and put them in a medium-sized saucepan with the sugar and ½ cup water. Heat gently until the sugar dissolves, then bring to a boil. Remove from the heat and stir in the chocolate until melted.

2. Remove the orange strips and add the whiskey and coffee. Pour into two tall heatproof glasses.

3. Lightly whip the cream with 2 tablespoons orange juice and spoon over the coffee. Serve immediately.

FLOURLESS CHOCOLATE CAKE P142

WITH A TWIST

SWEET CHOCOLATE SUSHI

This is a stunning variation on the familiar savory sushi. It is fun to make and a great after-dinner treat, particularly for those who prefer less-sweet chocolate flavors.

MAKES 25-30
- 1 kiwifruit, skinned
- ½ small mango, skinned
- 3 tablespoons tequila or vodka
- 1 cup Japanese sushi rice
- 14 oz can coconut milk
- 7 tablespoons superfine sugar
- 1 tablespoon white wine vinegar
- 3½ oz dark chocolate, broken into pieces

1. Cut the fruits into ¼-inch thick sticks and mix them with the liqueur. Put the rice in a heavy-bottom saucepan with the coconut milk. Bring to a boil, then simmer very gently for 10 minutes, stirring frequently, until the rice has the consistency of a thick risotto. Add the sugar and vinegar, cover, and let cool.

2. Melt the chocolate (see page 7). Draw three rectangles, each 9½ x 4 inches, on three sheets of nonstick parchment paper so that one long side is on the edge of the paper. Spread the chocolate over them.

3. Spoon the cooled rice onto three separate sheets of paper, spreading each to 9½ x 3¼ inches and pressing down very firmly with the back of a wetted spoon. Arrange a thin line of fruit down the center of each, reserving the juices.

4. Carefully roll up the fruits and rice in the paper, squeezing the edges of the paper tightly together so that the rice is tightly packed. Roll up the rice in the chocolate. (The chocolate edges should just meet.) Chill for 2 hours, then remove the paper.

5. Use a serrated knife to cut the sushi into logs. Drizzle with the reserved juices.

CHOCOLATE & BANANA SAMOSAS

These sweet samosas are filled with a winning combination—banana and chocolate—and are delicious hot, straight from the oven. Serve with lightly whipped cream or ice cream.

SERVES 12

- 2 ripe bananas, coarsely mashed
- ½ cup dark chocolate chips
- 12 phyllo pastry sheets, each about 12 x 7 inches
- Melted butter, for brushing
- Confectioners' sugar, for dusting

1. Preheat the oven to 350ºF. Line a baking sheet with parchment paper.

2. In a medium bowl, mix the bananas with the chocolate chips. Set aside.

3. Fold each sheet of phyllo pastry in half lengthwise. Place a large spoonful of the banana mixture at one end of the phyllo strip and then fold the corner of the phyllo over the mixture, covering it in a triangular shape. Continue folding the pastry over along the length of the strip of pastry to make a neat triangular samosa.

4. Moisten the edge with water to seal and place on the prepared baking sheet. Repeat with the remaining filling and pastry.

5. Brush the samosas with melted butter and bake in the oven for 12–15 minutes, or until lightly golden and crispy. Remove from the parchment paper, dust with confectioners' sugar, and serve hot.

TIP

- When working with phyllo pastry, always keep the pastry covered with a damp dish towel to prevent it from drying out, until ready to use.

CHOCOLATE GINGERBREAD PEOPLE

There is a homely appeal about baking a batch of gingerbread people. Their simple, chubby shapes will be appreciated by young and old alike, especially as they have chocolate clothes.

MAKES 10-20, DEPENDING ON SIZE

- 2½ cups all-purpose flour
- ¼ cup unsweetened cocoa
- 2 teaspoons ground ginger
- 1 teaspoon baking soda
- ½ cup (1 stick) unsalted butter or margarine, plus extra for greasing
- ¾ cup superfine sugar
- 4 teaspoons corn syrup or black treacle
- 1 egg
- 2 oz milk chocolate, broken into pieces
- 2 oz dark chocolate, broken into pieces

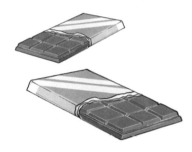

1. Preheat the oven to 375°F. Lightly grease two baking sheets.

2. Sift the flour, cocoa, ginger, and baking soda into a bowl. Cut the butter or margarine into small pieces and rub in using your fingertips until the mixture resembles bread crumbs.

3. Add the sugar, syrup or treacle, and egg and mix to form a firm dough. Knead until smooth. Roll out half the mixture on a lightly floured surface and cut out shapes, using a gingerbread cutter. Transfer to a baking sheet and bake in the oven for about 15 minutes until just beginning to darken around the edges. Repeat with the remaining dough. Leave the batches on the baking sheets for 3 minutes, then transfer to a wire rack to cool.

4. Melt the milk chocolate and dark chocolate separately (see page 7). Use the chocolate to decorate the cookies, spooning on "clothes" with a teaspoon, and piping features and buttons using a pastry bag. Allow to set.

TRIPLE CHOCOLATE PRETZELS

These dainty morsels are brushed with traditional salt glaze, baked, and drizzled with dark, white, and milk chocolate, making cute petits fours.

MAKES 40

- Scant 2 cups bread flour
- 1 teaspoon instant dried yeast
- 2 teaspoons superfine sugar
- Large pinch of salt
- 1 tablespoon melted butter or sunflower oil, plus extra for greasing
- Scant ½ cup warm water
- 3 oz each dark, white, and milk chocolate, broken into pieces

Glaze
- 2 tablespoons water
- ½ teaspoon salt

1. Lightly grease two large baking sheets.

2. Mix the flour, yeast, sugar, and salt in a bowl. Add the melted butter or oil and gradually mix in the warm water until you have a smooth dough. Knead the dough for 5 minutes on a lightly floured surface until smooth and elastic.

3. Cut the dough into quarters, then cut each quarter into 10 smaller pieces. Shape each piece into a thin rope about 8 inches long. Bend the rope so that it forms a wide arc, then bring one of the ends round in a loop and secure about halfway along the rope. Do the same with the other end, looping it across the first secured end.

4. Transfer the pretzels to the greased baking sheets. Cover loosely with lightly oiled plastic wrap and leave in a warm place for 30 minutes until well risen. Preheat the oven to 400°F.

5. To make the glaze, mix the water and salt in a bowl until the salt has dissolved, then brush this over the pretzels. Bake in the oven for 6–8 minutes until golden brown. Transfer to a wire rack and let cool.

6. Melt the dark, white, and milk chocolates in three separate bowls (see page 7). Using a spoon, drizzle random lines of dark chocolate over the pretzels. Allow to harden, then repeat with the white and then the milk chocolate. When set, transfer to an airtight container and eat within 2 days.

CHOCOLATE, ALMOND & FIG TART

SERVES 6-8

- ½ cup (1 stick) butter
- ¼ cup sugar
- 3 egg yolks
- 2 tablespoons extra virgin olive oil
- 1¾ cups all-purpose flour, sifted, plus extra for dusting
- ½ cup ground almonds
- Crème fraîche or sour cream, to serve

Filling
- 5 oz good-quality dark chocolate
- 1 tablespoon unsweetened cocoa, plus extra for dusting
- Pinch of salt
- ⅓ cup (⅔ stick) butter
- 2 tablespoons extra virgin olive oil
- 2 large egg yolks, plus 3 large eggs
- ⅔ cup superfine sugar
- 3 tablespoons heavy cream
- 2 tablespoons Amaretto di Saronno liqueur
- 3 fresh figs, halved
- 1 tablespoon slivered almonds, toasted

1. Preheat the oven to 350°F. To make the pastry, beat together the butter and sugar until pale, then beat in the egg yolks and olive oil. Mix in the flour and ground almonds and work together until you have a soft dough. Wrap loosely in plastic wrap and chill in the refrigerator for 1 hour.

2. Roll out the dough on a lightly floured board until it is slightly bigger than a 9-inch fluted tart pan. Lift the dough into the pan, pressing it so it rises up the side. Cover and chill in the refrigerator for 30 minutes.

3. Cover the bottom of the tart with waxed paper and fill it with ceramic pie weights. Bake blind in the oven for 15 minutes. Remove the paper and weights and return the pastry shell to the oven for another 5 minutes until it is crisp and lightly golden. Remove the pastry shell but leave the oven on.

4. Melt the chocolate with the cocoa, salt, butter, and olive oil (see page 7). Remove the pan from the heat and let the melted chocolate cool.

5. Beat the egg yolks, eggs, and sugar until pale and creamy. Fold the chocolate into the egg mixture and stir in the heavy cream and Amaretto. Pour the mixture into the pastry shell and arrange the halved figs on the top. Sprinkle with the slivered almonds, then return the tart to the oven for 30–35 minutes until just set. Serve warm, dusted with cocoa, with crème fraîche.

CHOCOLATE, MERINGUE & STRAWBERRY CAKE

SERVES 12

- ½ cup (1 stick) unsalted butter, softened, plus extra for greasing
- ½ cup superfine sugar
- 2 eggs
- ¾ cup self-rising flour
- 1 teaspoon baking powder
- 2 teaspoons vanilla extract
- ¼ cup unsweetened cocoa

Meringue
- 3 egg whites
- ¾ cup superfine sugar
- ¼ slivered almonds

To finish
- 1¼ cups heavy cream
- 3½ oz dark chocolate, broken into pieces
- 1½ cups strawberries

1. Preheat the oven to 350°F. Grease the bottoms and sides of two 8-inch round loose-bottom cake pans and line with nonstick parchment paper.

2. Put the butter, sugar, eggs, flour, baking powder, vanilla extract, and cocoa in a bowl and beat well until smooth and creamy. Turn the batter into the prepared pans and level the surface.

3. For the meringue, whisk the egg whites until stiff. Gradually whisk in the sugar, beating well after each addition until the mixture is stiff and glossy. Arrange half the almonds around the inside of the pans so they are flat against the paper, tucking them down between the cake batter and the paper.

4. Turn the meringue into the pans. Level the surface and sprinkle with the remaining almonds. Bake in the oven for about 35 minutes until the meringue is pale golden and just firm. Let cool in the pans.

5. Bring 6 tablespoons of the cream to a boil in a saucepan. Remove from the heat and stir in the chocolate. Leave until melted, then stir until smooth. Transfer to a bowl and let cool.

6. Reserve several whole strawberries for the top of the cake. Halve the remainder. Remove the cakes from the pans. Place one cake on a serving plate. Whip the remaining cream and spread over the cake on the plate. Arrange the halved strawberries on top. Lightly whip the chocolate cream until slightly thickened, then spread over the cake. Position the second cake on top and decorate with the reserved whole strawberries.

CHOCOLATE ROSE ROULADE

SERVES 8
- 6 oz dark chocolate, broken into pieces
- 5 eggs, separated
- ½ cup plus 2 tablespoons superfine sugar, plus extra for sprinkling
- 1¼ cups whipping cream
- 2 tablespoons rose water
- 1 tablespoon confectioners' sugar, plus extra for dusting
- Butter, for greasing
- Chocolate curls, to decorate (see page 9)

1. Preheat the oven to 350°F. Grease and line a 13 x 9-inch jelly roll pan with wax paper, then grease the paper.

2. Melt the chocolate (see page 7).

3. Whisk together the egg yolks and sugar until pale and creamy. Stir in the melted chocolate. Whisk the egg whites until stiff. Using a large metal spoon, fold the egg whites into the chocolate mixture. Turn into the prepared pan and spread to the corners. Bake in the oven for about 20 minutes until risen and just firm.

4. Sprinkle a sheet of wax paper with superfine sugar. Invert the roulade onto the paper and peel away the lining paper. Cover with a damp dish towel and let cool.

5. Whip the cream with the rose water and confectioners' sugar until softly peaking. Spread the mixture over the roulade and roll up from a short side. Place the roulade, join-side down, onto a serving plate. Scatter chocolate curls over the roulade and dust with confectioners' sugar.

FLOURLESS CHOCOLATE CAKE

SERVES 8

- 10 oz dark chocolate, broken into pieces
- ¾ cup (1½ sticks) butter
- 2 teaspoons vanilla extract
- 5 eggs
- 6 tablespoons heavy cream, plus extra to serve (optional)
- 1 cup golden baker's sugar (or superfine)
- Handful of blueberries
- Handful of raspberries

1. Preheat the oven to 350°F. Line the bottom and sides of a 9-inch cake pan with nonstick parchment paper.

2. Melt the chocolate with the butter (see page 7), stirring until the mixture is smooth. Remove from the heat and add the vanilla extract.

3. Beat the eggs, cream, and sugar for 3–4 minutes (the mixture will remain fairly runny), then fold into the chocolate mixture.

4. Pour the batter into the prepared pan and bake in the oven for 45 minutes, or until the top forms a crust. Allow the cake to cool and then run a knife around the edges to loosen it from the pan.

5. Turn out the cake onto a serving plate and top with a mixture of blueberries and raspberries. Serve with extra cream, if desired.

STICKY UPSIDE-DOWN PUDDING

An old-fashioned pudding that always looks impressive when turned out to reveal pretty pieces of pineapple, bathed in corn syrup.

SERVES 6

- 7 tablespoons corn syrup
- 14 oz can pineapple rings
- 7 oz dark chocolate, broken into pieces
- ½ cup (1 stick) unsalted butter or margarine, melted, plus extra for greasing
- 2 eggs
- 3 tablespoons superfine sugar
- 1 oz stem ginger from a jar (about 2 pieces), chopped
- 1 cup self-rising flour
- ¼ cup unsweetened cocoa
- Vanilla ice cream or custard, to serve

1. Preheat the oven to 375°F. Grease a 7½-cup shallow ovenproof dish and line the bottom with wax paper.

2. Spoon the corn syrup over the bottom of the dish. Thoroughly drain the pineapple rings and arrange them over the syrup. Melt the chocolate (see page 7), then stir in the butter or margarine and let cool slightly.

3. Put the eggs, sugar, stem ginger, and melted chocolate mixture in a bowl. Sift the flour and cocoa into the bowl. Beat well until smooth and creamy. Spoon the batter over the pineapple and level the surface.

4. Bake in the oven for 35–40 minutes until just firm in the center. Leave for 5 minutes, then invert onto a serving plate. Remove the wax paper. Serve with ice cream or custard.

TIP

- This recipe works equally well with canned apricots or pears, arranged cut-side down. You can also add a handful of chopped nuts or golden raisins to the cake batter, or use maple syrup instead of the corn syrup.

CHOCOLATE CARDAMOM RICE PUDDING

Cardamom adds an exotic flavor to even the simplest of dishes, so this is a perfect choice if you are looking for more adventurous chocolate combinations. It can be made equally successfully without the cardamom

SERVES 4
- 1 tablespoon green cardamom pods
- 2½ cups milk
- 3½ oz dark chocolate, broken into pieces
- ¼ cup pudding rice
- 3 tablespoons superfine sugar
- Butter, for greasing

1. Preheat the oven to 300°F. Lightly butter a 6-cup ovenproof dish.

2. Pound the cardamom pods using a mortar and pestle to release their seeds. Discard the pods and crush the seeds until broken down a little.

3. Bring the milk almost to a boil in a saucepan. Remove from the heat, add the chocolate, rice, sugar, and cardamom seeds and stir well. Leave for a couple of minutes to allow the chocolate to melt, then stir until combined.

4. Pour into the prepared dish and bake in the oven for 1½ hours or until the rice is tender. Serve warm.

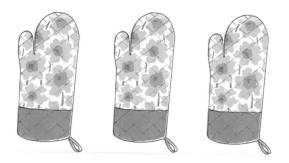

ROAST PHEASANT WITH SALSA AGRODOLCE

A salsa agrodolce is a sweet-sour sauce that here is enriched with a touch of dark chocolate.

SERVES 6

- 3 small hen pheasants
- 4 tablespoons (½ stick) butter, softened
- Small bunch of fresh thyme, plus 2 tablespoons chopped fresh thyme, to serve
- Salt and freshly ground black pepper

Salsa agrodolce
- 1 tablespoon (⅛ stick) butter

- 1 onion, finely chopped
- 2 tablespoons superfine sugar
- 3 tablespoons red wine vinegar
- ¾ cup red wine
- ⅔ cup chicken stock
- ½ oz dark chocolate (80% cocoa solids), broken into pieces
- 2 tablespoons (¼ stick) unsalted butter

1. Preheat the oven to 375°F.

2. Place the pheasants in a large roasting pan and rub over the butter. Stuff each cavity with the thyme sprigs and season well with salt and pepper. Roast for about 50–55 minutes or until a toothpick inserted into the leg joint feels piping hot. Remove from the oven, cover, and let rest for 10 minutes.

3. While the pheasants are roasting you can make the salsa agrodolce. Melt the butter in a small saucepan and add the onion. Cook slowly for 10 minutes until the onions are softened but not colored. Spoon into a bowl and set aside.

4. In the same pan add the superfine sugar and red wine vinegar. Over a gentle heat stir until the sugar has dissolved, then turn the heat up and boil until the liquid has reduced to almost nothing. Pour in the wine and stock, add the reserved onions, and simmer for 15 minutes. Take off the heat and whisk in the chocolate followed by the unsalted butter. Taste the sauce and season with salt and plenty of pepper.

5. Serve slices of the pheasant with a little sauce and chopped thyme scattered over to finish.

BAKED HAM WITH CHOCOLATE GLAZE

This is an interesting and delicious alternative to the traditional honey and mustard glaze for ham. I prefer this version served cold with a crunchy salad and baked potato.

SERVES 6

- 6 lb piece unsmoked ham, bone-in
- 1 onion
- 1 celery stick
- 1 carrot, peeled and halved
- 1 teaspoon whole cloves

Glaze
- ⅔ cup light brown sugar
- ⅓ cup cider vinegar
- ¼ cup ginger wine
- 1½ oz dark chocolate (70% cocoa solids), broken into pieces
- Pinch of ground cloves
- Salt and freshly ground black pepper

1. Put the ham into a large saucepan and cover with water. Bring to a boil and then remove from the heat and drain.

2. Cover with cold water and add the onion, celery, carrot, and cloves. Bring to a boil, then turn the heat down and simmer for 2 hours.

3. Meanwhile, make the glaze. Put the sugar, vinegar, and ginger wine into a saucepan and slowly bring to a boil. Simmer for 5 minutes.

4. Take off the heat and whisk in the chocolate. Season with a little salt and pepper and stir in the ground cloves.

5. Preheat the oven to 375°F. Drain the ham and put it in a large roasting pan.

6. Pour the chocolate glaze over the gammon. Roast in the oven for 20 minutes, basting the meat every 5 minutes with the chocolate glaze. Remove from the oven and let rest for 10–15 minutes before serving.

BRAISED LAMB SHANKS WITH VEGETABLES

SERVES 6

- 6 lamb shanks
- 2 onions
- 8 thyme sprigs
- 2 bay leaves
- 2 teaspoons unsweetened cocoa
- 1¾ cups red wine
- 3 garlic cloves
- 1 teaspoon black peppercorns
- 4 tablespoons olive oil
- 7 oz baby carrots
- 1 cup fava beans
- 6 pickled walnuts, halved
- 1 oz dark chocolate, chopped
- Parsley, to garnish
- Salt

1. Put the lamb shanks in a large, shallow container in which they fit quite snugly. Roughly chop one of the onions and put in a blender or food processor with the herbs, cocoa, wine, garlic, and peppercorns. Blend until slightly pulpy and pour over the lamb. Cover and allow to marinate for 24–48 hours, turning the meat several times.

2. Preheat the oven to 325°F. Drain the lamb, reserving the marinade, and pat the meat dry on paper towels. Heat the oil in a large skillet and fry the lamb for about 10 minutes, turning frequently until deep golden. Transfer the meat to a shallow ovenproof dish or roasting pan.

3. Finely chop the remaining onion and fry in the pan for 3 minutes. Strain the marinade into the pan and bring to a boil. Pour it over the lamb and cover the dish with a lid or foil. Cook in the oven for 1½ hours or until the lamb is tender.

4. Scatter the carrots, beans, and pickled walnuts around the lamb and return to the oven for an additional 15 minutes or until the vegetables are tender.

5. Drain the meat and vegetables and transfer to serving plates. Stir the chocolate into the pan juices until melted. Check the seasoning and pour the sauce into a pitcher. Serve the lamb drizzled with the sauce and garnished with parsley.

CHOCOLATE & PEPPERED STEAK

Try and find some flavorsome, well-hung meats for this dish. Tenderloin steak may be the most tender, but it is often lacking in flavor.

SERVES 2
- 2 x 7 oz sirloin steaks at room temperature
- 1 teaspoon sunflower oil
- 1 tablespoon crushed black peppercorns
- ½ tablespoon grated dark chocolate (at least 80% cocoa solids)
- Salt

1. Put the steaks onto a plate and brush with the oil. Press the peppercorns evenly over both sides and season with salt.

2. Heat a skillet until hot and fry the steaks for 1-2 minutes each side, depending on their thickness and how well done you like them.

3. Remove the steaks to serving plates and sprinkle over the chocolate. Let rest for a couple of minutes, then serve.

TIP

- Never be afraid to let any meat, red or white, rest. It allows it to relax as the juices disperse, and this helps the meat to retain its moisture.

ROAST CHICKEN WITH BITTER CHOCOLATE GRAVY

Perfect with roast chicken, Bitter Chocolate Gravy is more of a jus than the thicker traditional gravy. It is quite a strong sauce, so a little goes a long way.

SERVES 4-5

- 1 lemon, cut into quarters
- 1 free-range chicken, weighing about 4 lb
- Half a head of garlic, separated into cloves, unpeeled
- 1 small bunch of fresh thyme
- 6 tablespoons (¾ stick) butter, slightly softened
- 2¼ cups chicken stock
- 1 tablespoon balsamic vinegar
- 1 oz dark chocolate (70% cocoa solids), broken into pieces
- Salt and freshly ground black pepper

1. Preheat the oven to 375°F.

2. Stuff the lemon quarters into the chicken cavity along with the garlic cloves and half the thyme. Smear 4 tablespoons (½ stick) of the butter over the chicken and season with salt and pepper.

3. Place the chicken in a large roasting pan and cover with foil. Roast for 50 minutes, then remove the foil, baste, and continue to cook for 20–25 minutes. The chicken is done when the juices from the center of the leg run clear. Remove the chicken from the roasting pan, cover with foil, and let rest for 10–15 minutes.

4. Remove the leaves from the remaining thyme sprigs and chop finely. Pour off the fat from the roasting pan, leaving the juices, and add the chopped thyme. Over a high heat add the chicken stock and balsamic vinegar and simmer for 5 minutes. Take off the heat, whisk in the chocolate, and stir until smooth.

5. Taste and season with salt and pepper. Whisk in the remaining 2 tablespoons (¼ stick) butter. Serve with the roast chicken.

MEXICAN
CHICKEN MOLE

- -

This Mexican dish is renowned for the subtle addition of chocolate in the spicy, nutty sauce. It is a good party dish as quantities can easily double up.

SERVES 4

- 3 tablespoons olive oil
- 1 oven-ready chicken, about 2¾ lb
- 1 large onion, quartered, plus 1 onion, roughly chopped
- 4 garlic cloves, halved
- 2½ cups water
- 1 red chili, seeded and roughly chopped
- 1 teaspoon cumin seeds
- ½ teaspoon ground cinnamon
- ¼ teaspoon ground cloves
- 5 tablespoons blanched almonds
- 2 tablespoons sesame seeds
- 1 corn or wheat tortilla, about 1½ oz, torn into pieces
- ½ oz dark chocolate, chopped
- Small handful of fresh cilantro leaves, chopped
- Salt

1. Preheat the oven to 375°F.

2. Heat 2 tablespoons of the oil in a large flameproof casserole and fry the chicken until golden. Add the quartered onion, garlic, water, and a little salt. Bring to a boil, and cover. Bake for about 1 hour until cooked through.

3. Meanwhile, start the sauce. Heat the remaining oil in a skillet and fry the chopped onion and chili for 3 minutes, stirring. Add the spices and fry gently for an additional 2 minutes.

4. Put the almonds, sesame seeds, and tortilla into a food processor and blend until coarsely ground. Add the contents of the skillet and blend to a smooth paste.

5. Transfer the chicken to a serving plate and keep warm. Measure 1¼ cups of the stock (reserving the remainder for another recipe) and add it to the processor. Blend until smooth and pour the sauce back into the skillet.

6. Stir in the chocolate and a little of the cilantro and heat gently until the chocolate has melted. Carve the chicken and serve with the sauce, with the remaining cilantro sprinkled over.

ITALIAN SWEET & SOUR CHICKEN

A dish to suit almost any occasion, from family supper to entertaining friends, this is ideal with polenta (cornmeal), which can be used to mop up the sweet, tangy chocolate juices.

SERVES 4

- 3 tablespoons olive oil
- 1 onion, finely chopped
- 2 oz lean smoked bacon, diced
- 2 teaspoons dark brown sugar
- 4 chicken thighs, skinned
- 4 chicken drumsticks, skinned
- 3 garlic cloves, crushed
- 2 bay leaves
- 6 tablespoons red wine vinegar
- 1¼ cups chicken stock
- ⅓ cup golden raisins
- 1½ oz dark chocolate, chopped
- ⅓ cup pine nuts, lightly toasted
- Salt and freshly ground black pepper

1. Heat the oil in a large heavy-bottom saucepan and gently fry the onion and bacon for 5 minutes until golden. Add the sugar and chicken and fry for an additional 5 minutes, turning the chicken frequently until it is golden.

2. Add the garlic, bay leaves, vinegar, and stock and bring to a boil. Reduce the heat, cover with a lid, and simmer very gently for 40 minutes or until the chicken is tender.

3. Drain the chicken and keep the pieces warm. Stir the golden raisins, chocolate, and half the pine nuts into the sauce and cook gently for 5 minutes. Season with salt and pepper to taste.

4. Arrange the chicken on serving plates and spoon over the sauce. Scatter over the remaining pine nuts and serve.

MARINATED DUCK WITH GINGER SAUCE

Although distinctively chocolaty, this fabulous sauce has a fresh tang that is the perfect complement for the richness of the duck.

SERVES 4

- 4 large duck breasts
- 1 onion, sliced
- 1 celery stick, chopped
- 4 tablespoons honey
- 2 oz fresh ginger, grated
- 3 tablespoons lemon juice
- 1 tablespoon soy sauce
- 2 teaspoons five spice powder
- 1 tablespoon peanut oil
- ½ oz dark chocolate, chopped

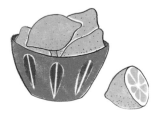

1. Score each piece of duck several times with a sharp knife. Scatter the onion and celery in a shallow dish and place the duck on top.

2. Mix together the honey, ginger, lemon juice, soy sauce, and five spice powder and pour it over the duck. Cover and allow to marinate in the refrigerator for at least 6 hours or overnight, turning once.

3. Preheat the oven to 350°F. Drain the duck and strain the marinade into a small bowl. Pat the duck dry on paper towels. Heat the oil in a heavy-bottom skillet and fry the duck pieces, skin side down, for 5 minutes until dark golden.

4. Transfer to a roasting pan and cook in the oven for about 30 minutes until tender. Transfer the duck to a warmed dish and drain off all the fat from the pan.

5. Add the reserved marinade to the pan and bring it to a boil. Reduce the heat and stir in the chocolate to make a smooth, glossy sauce. Spoon over the duck on warmed serving plates.

INDEX